GALATIANS

A Verse by Verse Study

GALATIANS

A Verse by Verse Study

Herschel H. Hobbs

WORD BOOKS
PUBLISHER
4800 WEST WACO DRIVE
WACO, TEXAS
76703

GALATIANS

ISBN 0-8499-0070-0
Library of Congress catalog card number: 77-92467
Printed in the United States of America

For information on Scripture versions used, see page 6.

Dedicated to the memory of

M. E. DODD

*a masterful preacher of the gospel
of salvation by grace through faith.*

Contents

Introduction

GALATIANS is a trumpet blast for freedom in Christ. It furnished the battle cry of Martin Luther in the Protestant Reformation. It is one of the "big four" (Romans, 1 and 2 Corinthians, Galatians) whose authenticity as epistles of Paul have never been seriously questioned, except by the most radical critics. It is a letter which is much needed today in a world that is overrun by various approaches to the gospel, and by "isms" which point away from Christ into the "never-never land" of non-Christian ways to find peace of mind and soul.

The purpose of this volume is not to delve deeply into the various critical problems concerning Galatians. Anyone who is interested in such may find discussion of them in any standard commentary on the book. Other scholarly works are available beyond that.[1] My purpose is to seek to interpret Galatians itself. It is an endeavor to present the fruits of scholarship without laborious details of such. An attempt will be made to see the book's message in its original historical setting, and apply its truths to similar matters in today's world.

Date, Origin, and Destination

The questions of the date, origin, and destination of Galatians are matters of disagreement among interpreters. The first two hinge largely on the third. So actually we must work backward in deciding these issues.

The word *Galatia* comes from the word *Gaul.* In his *Expository Sermons on Galatians,* W. A. Criswell (p. 14) notes that the letter might just as well read, "To the churches of Gaul in Asia Minor, not the Gaul of Western Europe." In the third century B.C., Gauls from Europe settled in a portion of Asia Minor. Their kingdom came to be known as Galatia. In 25 B.C. it fell to Rome, and was called the Roman province of Galatia. In Paul's first missionary journey (Acts 13–14) he and Barnabas established churches in Pisidian Antioch, Iconium, Lystra, and Derbe. These were in this province.

The question of destination has resulted in two

---

1. See Donald Guthrie (pp. 72–91); Werner Georg Kümmel (pp. 190–98); A. H. McNeile (pp. 143–45). Full information is given in the bibliography on these and all books referred to in the text by author.

schools of thought. One holds that the letter was written to churches in North Galatia which Paul established at the beginning of his second missionary journey (Acts 16:6; see 18:23). These hold that the
churches were not in the original province of Galatia,
but were ethnological Galatians. Luke mentions no
such churches. The tone of Acts 16:6–8 suggests a
hurried journey.

The other group holds that these churches are the
ones mentioned in Acts 13–14 which were in South
Galatia: Pisidian Antioch, Lystra, Iconium, Derbe,
and perhaps others. This seems to be the more practi-
cal view.

As to the place of origin, some hold that this is
Paul's first letter, and was written from Antioch of
Syria (Acts 15:35–36) or even on the way back to
Antioch from the Jerusalem Conference (Acts 15).
Others see Ephesus (Acts 19) or Macedonia (Acts
20:1) as the place of writing. The latter would place
Galatians just after 2 Corinthians which was written
from Macedonia. Still others see Corinth as the place
of writing. It seems that a better case can be made for
Corinth than for the others.

Those who hold to Corinth as the place of origin
for this letter see it as written just before Romans.
This would date it in late 56 or early 57 A.D.

Reason and Purpose

Paul's reason for writing Galatians is bound to his
purpose. The thing which prompted Galatians also
determined its purpose.

In Acts 15:1 we read that "certain men which came down from Judaea taught the brethren [in Antioch of Syria], and said, Except ye be circumcised after the manner of Moses, ye cannot be saved." Who were these men? They were Judaizers, or, as I call them, *Jew-makers.* They were Jews who had adopted the Christian faith, but who held on to their old Jewish practices.

Judaism taught that only Jews could be saved. So, said the Judaizers, for a Gentile to be saved he must first become a Jew in religion. This involved being circumcised, making certain sacrifices, and living by the Mosaic law. Paul and Barnabas had been on a mission to the Gentiles. They had preached salvation by grace through faith in Jesus Christ. The Judaizers taught a salvation by works plus faith, or legalism plus faith. This was the very opposite of what Paul and Barnabas had been preaching. They taught that Gentiles could be saved as Gentiles. The Judaizers taught that they must be saved as Jews.

Naturally the Christians in Antioch were upset. But no more so than Paul when he learned about this upon his return to Antioch. The result was the first conference held in the Christian movement. Since the meeting was held in Jerusalem, it is called the Jerusalem Conference (Acts 15:2–29). The problem involved people of both churches: Antioch and Jerusalem. So representatives of the church in Antioch went to Jerusalem. The entire conference was held under the guidance of the Holy Spirit (Acts 15:28). The very gospel itself was at stake.

The conference decided the matter in favor of the gospel of grace through faith. But this did not end the matter. When the Judaizers lost out on doctrine, they attacked Paul himself. They said that he was not a true apostle. According to them he received his understanding of the gospel from others, and then twisted it to his own ends. They accused him of preaching for money, and said that he did not love the people with whom he worked. Also they made light of his personal appearance and his method of preaching the gospel. All of these things are reflected in certain of his writings, especially Galatians and the Corinthian epistles.

Paul had largely dealt with the Judaizer problem in Corinth through his two letters to that church. But apparently upon arriving in Corinth (Acts 20:2–3), he learned of the trouble that this heretical group was causing in the churches of Galatia. He had spent about three years in Ephesus (Acts 20:31). During this time the Judaizers had been busy in Galatia since Paul's previous visit there (Acts 18:23). So evidently early in his brief stay of three months in Corinth (Acts 20:3), he wrote this letter. Someone has said that he wrote it with a blazing pen. Of course, he dictated the letter as was his custom. But he must have dictated it with great passion. Then in his own hand he wrote the concluding words (Gal. 6:11–18). He wanted to remove any possibility that the Judaizers might claim that the letter was not from Paul.

Thus Paul's purpose in writing Galatians was to refute the teachings of the Judaizers and their charges made against him. It was to prevent Gentile Christians from becoming slaves to legalism, and to establish them in their freedom in Christ.

While in Corinth Paul planned that after a brief visit to Jerusalem he would go to Spain. On his way he would pay a visit to the church in Rome (Rom. 15:23–25). So before leaving for Jerusalem he wrote Romans. Since he had never visited Rome, though he had friends there whom he had known elsewhere (Rom. 16), in Romans he sets forth the gospel as he preached it. It is the most complete exposition of the gospel in the New Testament (see my *Romans: A Verse by Verse Study* [Waco: Word, 1977]). Its similarity to Galatians is quite evident, though it is a more expanded treatment of the gospel. Also it is presented in a quieter, more reasoned style than that found in Galatians. This argues for the position that Galatians was written just prior to Romans. Indeed, Romans 16:17–18 probably is a warning to be on the alert concerning the Judaizers should they come to Rome.

Present Theological Value

Galatians has a message for every generation, including ours. When reduced to a simple statement, the teaching of the Judaizers is salvation by *works plus faith* in Jesus Christ. By whatever name it may be called, any Christian group which teaches that one is saved by faith plus works is a descendant of the Judaizers. Anything which adds works to salvation cancels out grace. For basically grace means a gift which is received not by merit but as an expression of God's redeeming love.

Freedom is the watchword of the present hour. And freedom is not something granted by man. It is a right conferred by God. This is true of all freedom, but especially is it true of the message of the gospel. No person is truly free until he is made free in Jesus Christ (John 8:32, 36). Grace is free, but it also makes its demands in godly living and service for God through serving men (Rom. 6). One does not do good works in order to be saved. But he should do them because he is saved (Eph. 2:8–10).

The clarion call down the ages is "Stand fast therefore in the liberty wherewith Christ hath made us free, and be not entangled again with the yoke of bondage" (Gal. 5:1).

1

In Defense of the Gospel

Galatians 1

PAUL could be broadminded as to the motive out of which one preached Christ, so long as Christ was preached in the full meaning of the word (Phil. 1:15–18). But he was extremely narrow-minded as to the truth of the gospel. What his opponents did to him as a person did not matter. But when attacks upon him were made for the purpose of discounting the gospel he preached, that was something else. Already in 2 Corinthians 10–12 in classic irony he had refuted charges made against him in Corinth by the Judaizers. Upon his arrival in that city he learned of the havoc being wrought by these false teachers in the churches of Galatia. And since his plans made it impossible for him to visit them, he dashed off a letter to them that he might strengthen them in their faith.

These churches were composed largely of Gentiles who had become Christians through faith in Jesus Christ, without having gone through Judaism. So they were greatly disturbed by the teachings of the Judaizers. If the Judaizers were right, then they were not saved at all—Paul had misled them. Thus it is understandable that the apostle would, after a curt salutation, move in immediately to deal with the problem.

Since Paul himself had been made the center of the problem by the Judaizers, Galatians 1 and 2 are very personal in nature. The apostle was hesitant to boast about himself (2 Cor. 12:11), but he did not hesitate to do so if it involved the validity of the gospel (2 Cor. 11:1–31).

Salutation (1:1–5)

This salutation is unique in Paul's writings. Only here does he fail to express thanks for his readers, which shows how troubled and hurt he is over news of the Galatians' defection, or danger of doing so, from the true gospel which they had received from him.

"Paul, an apostle." The Greek phrase is terse (*Paulos apostolos*). In his commentary, John W. Mac-Gorman notes that "the argument begins dramatically with the second word of the original text!" (p. 52). Since the Judaizers were attacking his gospel on the basis that he was not a true apostle, he responds immediately with a denial of their charge. They claimed that he was not one of the twelve apostles appointed to that office by Jesus, and that his *claimed* apostleship was received by appointment from men—perhaps from Peter. He touches upon this matter later (1:18, 2:11–14).

The Greek word translated *apostle* means *one sent forth*. It applied originally to the Twelve. Prior to Pentecost, following the suicide of Judas, Matthias was chosen by "lots" to fill this vacated place (Acts 1:15–26). Since this choice was made by "lots," something like drawing straws, and prior to the coming of the Holy Spirit in power at Pentecost, it is my feeling that Matthias was men's choice, not that of the Lord. We never hear of Matthias again. It seems that Paul was the Lord's choice to fill this vacancy.

In the first century the office of apostle carried with it a special authority in spiritual matters. Barnabas and others were called apostles, though not in this sense. They were simply sent forth to preach the gospel. In Ephesians 4:11, "apostles" refers to one of the gifts the ascended Christ gave to his churches. Here the word seems to carry the idea of *missionaries,* a word which comes from the Latin equivalent of the Greek *apostolos,* one sent forth. The apostles seem to have been pioneers who planted the gospel in areas where it had not been preached previously (Rom. 15:20). But the office seems not to have carried the authority attached to it originally.

However, Paul insists that his apostleship ranked in importance with that of the original Twelve. True, he had not been with Jesus during his earthly ministry. But he did claim, and rightly so, that he had seen him after his resurrection (Acts 1:21–22; 9:3–6, 15; 1 Cor.

9:1–2; 15:8). His experiences with Christ had been such that he could claim companionship with Christ in the Lord's work (2 Cor. 11:23–31).

Therefore, Paul is insistent that his apostleship is "not of [from] men, neither by [through] man, but by [through] Jesus Christ, and God the Father, who raised him from the dead." Note the emphatic position of "not." He received his apostleship not from men (the Twelve?) or through any man (Peter?) as an intermediate agent. "But" sets in contrast the latter part of the statement from the former part. His appointment came directly from Jesus Christ and God the Father. The same Father who raised his Son from the dead made Paul an apostle, the Son being the intermediate agent ("by," translates *dia,* meaning through).

In the salutation the apostle includes the brethren who are with him, but he does not identify them (v. 2). Assuming that the letter was written either in Macedonia or Corinth, Floyd E. Hamilton suggests "probably Luke (Acts 20:6), Timothy, Erastus (Acts 19:22), and probably Gaius, Tychicus, and Trophimus. . . . Possibly Titus was also with him, having brought news of conditions in the churches of Galatia," (p. 9). Of course, this could include all the Christians in Corinth.

Having signed the letter, Paul now addresses it "unto the churches of Galatia" (v. 2). Note the plural "churches." These are the local churches in Pisidian Antioch, Iconium, Lystra, Derbe, and maybe others.

These were churches in the Roman province of Galatia.

The word translated *church* is *ekklēsia,* which means "the called out ones" or assembly. In Acts 19:32, 39–40 it is so translated, and refers to a local political group operating through democratic processes within the framework of the laws of the Roman Empire. This principle carries over into the idea of a local church operating through democratic processes under the lordship of Jesus Christ. It also is found in the sense of the congregation of Israel assembled before God in the wilderness and under his direct theocractic rule (Acts 7:38). In the Septuagint (the Greek translation of the Old Testament), it translates *qahal* meaning congregation. This sense carries over into the New Testament in some uses, for the general idea of the redeemed of all the ages (Eph. 1:1; 3:10; Col. 1:18) under God's direct theocratic rule. But out of 115 times it is used in the New Testament, at least 93 times it refers to a local church. The singular form is never used with reference to a group of churches. Hence the plural form here.

In verse 3 Paul says that his readers may have "grace" and "peace" which come from God the Father and our Lord Jesus Christ. *Grace (chairē)* and *peace* (Hebrew, *shalom*) were standard greetings used by Greeks and Jews respectively. However, here the word translated *grace* is *charis.* Thus the phrase is more than a simple greeting. Grace is God's gift or unmerited favor toward sinful men. It is at the heart of the gospel, as it distinguishes between the gospel and law or any code of conduct. It is God's gift rather than man's accomplishment.

Thus the order of the words is significant: *grace,* then *peace*—an inner calm even in a storm. We must receive God's grace before we can know his peace. This simple prayer spoke volumes to the original readers of Galatians, even as it does to us.

The mention of "our Lord Jesus Christ" leads Paul to declare for the first time in Galatians that which our Lord did for us. He is "the one giving himself for [*huper,* on behalf of, as a substitute] our sins, that he might deliver us from this present evil world" or age (v. 4, literal). This letter emphasizes the substitutionary atonement which Christ wrought according to God's will (2:20–21; 3:1, 13; 6:12, 14).

This is to be expected since Paul opposes legalism as being involved in salvation. MacGorman notes the failure of the Judaizers to see that Christ alone is sufficient for salvation. "Legalism never does! It is forever placing above the cross on which Christ died an inscription which reads: 'Necessary but not enough!' Thus it adds rites to faith, insisting that faith alone cannot avail" (p. 83).

The word translated *deliver* means to rescue. We were held in the tyrannical power of Satan, but Christ rescued us from it (Col. 1:13; same idea but a different verb). J. B. Lightfoot sees this idea as the keynote of Galatians. "The Gospel is a rescue, an emancipation from the state of bondage" (p. 73).

For this reason Paul closes his salutation by ascribing glory to God "for ever and ever," or "unto the ages of the ages." This is the strongest Greek expression for *eternity*. The Greek text has no verb. So it is an *absolute*. "Amen"—so be it—expresses the certainty that this will be true. God's created order declares his glory (Ps. 19:1). But his greatest glory is revealed in his redemptive work.

Paul's Warning against a False Gospel (1:6–10)

Following his salutation Paul moved immediately into the problem in Galatia. He wasted no words with a tactful approach. So to speak, he took off his gloves and grasped the issues. And why not, since the future of the gospel itself was at stake!

"I marvel that ye are so soon removed from him that called you into the grace of Christ unto another gospel: Which is not another; but there be some that trouble you, and would pervert the gospel of Christ" (vv. 6–7).

The word translated *marvel* expresses astonishment over something which one does not understand. Olaf M. Norlie in his *The New Testament: A New Translation* reads, "I am dumfounded." The present tense means that he is continuously dumfounded.* *Removed* trans-

---

* Since reference will be made to tenses, a word is necessary for those not versed in the Greek language. In Greek, tenses primarily refer to kinds of action, with time being secondary. The *present* tense expresses repeated or habitual action in the present. The *imperfect* tense connotes repeated action in past time. The *aorist* tense connotes repeated point action. It is the historical tense with no particular reference to time. "Aorist" *(a-oristos)* means undefined or without boundary. It means that something took place at a given point in time, with the context determining

lates a verb that means to change places or to transfer. The present middle (reflexive) voice means that the Galatians were doing this themselves as they succumbed to the false teachings of the Judaizers. The idea is that they were in the process of transferring their loyalty from Christ to the Mosaic law; that is they were doing this or were on the verge of doing so.

"So soon" could refer to the time since they first received the gospel, or since the Judaizers arrived on the scene. Assuming that the letter was written from Corinth, the latter is the preferred meaning.

The one calling, of course, is God. He calls "into" or rather "in the sphere of [en] the grace of Christ." If the readers desert this gospel of grace they are deserting both Christ and the Father. To be sure, God gave the Mosaic code. But his full revelation in Christ is one of grace, not law.

The teachings of the Judaizers are "another gospel." Here *another (heteron)* means another of a different kind. Paul hastens to add that it is not "another," and this Greek word means another of the same kind as that which Paul had preached. Law and grace are incompatible. Indeed, they cancel out each other. Since grace is a gift, it cannot be earned, else it would

---

the time. It may also express action as a whole. The *perfect* tense expresses perfected, completed, or intensive action in the past which continues into the present; or a past completed action whose results are still true at the time of speaking or writing. It supposes that such action will continue to be true. For further study see A. T. Robertson, *A Grammar of the Greek New Testament* (New York: Doran, 1923), pp. 821–910.

be that which is one's due. It would place God in man's debt, rather than placing man in God's debt.

If I should sell you a piece of property worth $10,000 for $1.00, you would get a bargain. But it would be a purchase and not a gift. So the message of the Judaizers is not a gospel of the same kind as Paul's; it is a gospel of a different kind.

For that matter, it is no *gospel* at all. The word *gospel* means good news. It is the good news that God by grace through his Son has provided salvation to all people who believe in Jesus. This depends upon God and not upon man. If my salvation depends upon what I do plus faith in Christ, then it is bad news. Because nothing that I do can merit salvation.

We often hear it said that we are all trying to get to heaven, but we are traveling different roads. This idea is born of sentiment, not Scripture. God has but one plan of salvation (Acts 15:11). It is not labeled Baptist, Methodist, Presbyterian, Lutheran, Catholic, or whatever. It is labeled "Grace through Faith in Christ" (Eph. 2:8–10).

Nevertheless, Paul notes that some are troubling the Galatians by trying to pervert or twist the gospel of Christ. The word translated *trouble* has in it the picture of an ocean caught in the teeth of a storm. This expresses the turbulent condition which existed in the churches of Galatia.

Then the apostle makes one of his strongest statements (vv. 8–9). "But though we [Paul], or an angel from heaven, preach any other gospel unto you than that which we have preached unto you, let him be accursed." And lest his readers think that he got carried away in his zeal in making such an extreme statement, he repeats it for emphasis (v. 9). However, there is a difference between the two statements. In the "if" clause, in verse 8 Paul uses the subjunctive mode of the verb. It expresses a condition which, though possible, is highly unlikely. In the "if" clause in verse 9 he uses the indicative mode. This means that it is actually happening as the Judaizers preach their false gospel.

Paul says in verse 8 (literal), "Just suppose that I, or even an angel from heaven, should preach to you a gospel different [*heteron*, v. 6] from the one I preached to you." *Preached* translates the verb meaning to evangelize or bear good news.

Paul imagines what he considers practically impossible: that he would return to these churches, and say, "I was wrong when I said that Gentiles can be saved by grace through faith. The Judaizers are right. You must be circumcised and live by Moses' law, then believe in Jesus, if you want to be saved." Or that a messenger from heaven itself should come, and say, "Do not listen to Paul. He is a renegade Jew, and does not know the true gospel. Listen instead to the Judaizers. For they have God's message for you."

The apostle says that if either of these should happen, "Let him be accursed!" *Accursed* translates the Greek *anathema*. The Septuagint uses *anathema* to translate the Hebrew word *cherem*, meaning a devoted thing, something so abominable to God that he is glorified by its destruction (cf. Deut. 7:24–26; Josh. 6:17–19; 7:1, 19–26; MacGorman, p. 84). This is a terrible curse which Paul calls down upon those who pervert the gospel. And as the indicative mode shows, he called down this curse upon the Judaizers themselves (v. 9).

Paul's words sound harsh and strange to many modern ears. The trend of this age is toward broadmindedness. We are told that we should dispense with our differences in theology, and major upon our points of agreement. But strangely they apply this only in matters of religion. No sane person wants a banker who says that two plus two equals three. Two plus two equals *four,* no more and no less. And all of our clever juggling of figures can never change that. We do not want a pharmacist who just throws together any drugs which may suit his fancy. We want him to follow exactly the doctor's prescription. This is true narrow-mindedness. We commend this quality in matters of lesser importance—finances and health. But many condemn it in matters of religion.

Paul was narrow-minded in how God proposes to save a lost humanity. Peter was likewise when he told his Jewish audience, "Neither is there salvation in any other: for there is none other name under heaven given among men, whereby we must be saved" (Acts 4:12; *must* translates a verb *(dei)* which expresses a moral and spiritual necessity). John the apostle of love was also narrow-minded when he said, "He that hath the Son hath life; and he that hath not the Son of God hath not life" (1 John 5:12). But they were only following Jesus who said, "Enter ye in at the strait gate: for wide is the gate, and broad is the way, that leadeth to [into the] destruction [hell], and many there be which go in thereat: Because strait is the gate, and narrow is the way, which leadeth unto [the] life, and few there be that find it" (Matt. 7:13–14). Where the eternal destiny of souls is involved, it is sin to be anything but narrow-minded.

Paul was as narrow-minded as the truth. A train is as narrow-minded as the rails upon which it moves. Otherwise it could not perform its purpose. Christians must be as narrow-minded as the truth about Christ. If there were many ways by which God saves men, Paul might well be called a bigot. But because he was convinced that there is only one way of salvation—by grace through faith in Christ—he was true to his calling in the extreme statement which he made. He would have been truant to his calling had he said any less. MacGorman rightly comments, "Many have a problem with Paul here, not because they fail to understand what he says, but simply because they do not believe what he believes. Not all of the *heteron* [of a different kind] gospels died in the first century!" (p. 85).

Many modern groups which deny the deity-humanity of Jesus Christ, or who teach salvation by faith plus works, like to trace their line back to the first century. But if they follow this line to its source, they must admit that their spiritual ancestors are those whom Paul, Peter, John, and others were opposing in their writings.

Paul justifies his position in verse 10. "For do I now persuade men, or God? or do I seek to please men? For if I yet pleased men, I should not be the servant of Christ."

Now refers back to verses 8 and 9. The Judaizers were accusing Paul of being a man-pleaser. *Persuade* is used in this sense. They said that when he was with Jews he taught circumcision (but see 2:3); but when he was with Gentiles he discounted circumcision and the Mosaic law (Acts 21:20–24). Paul denies such a charge. Surely if he were trying simply to please men, he would not have said what he had just written. If he were nothing more than a man-pleaser he would not be a true "servant" or slave *(doulos)* of Christ. He is only endeavoring to please God by being true to the gospel. And for this he paid a great price in suffering, as any servant of Christ should be willing to do in order to be true to his stewardship of the gospel.

Insistence upon His Apostleship (1:11–17)

The heart of the Judaizers' attack upon Paul centered in his apostleship. They denied that he was a true apostle. Also they insisted that he received his message from men rather than from God. Furthermore, they charged that he had even misunderstood or was deliberately misrepresenting that message. In speculating as to the charge that Paul's apostleship rested upon human authority, it has been suggested that the Judaizers pointed either to the Ananias incident in Damascus (Acts 9:10–19) or to the action of the church in Antioch in laying hands upon Barnabas and Saul (Acts 13:1–3). However, in these cases the action was taken at the command of Jesus and the Holy Spirit respectively. But as the context in Galatians shows, Paul is thinking about the apostles in Jerusalem. Looking ahead we note the progression of Paul's argument: "from independence of (1:11–24), to recognition by (2:1–10), to rebuke of (2:11–21) the Jerusalem apostles" (MacGorman, p. 86).

Paul continues his argument for his gospel and apostleship (they stand or fall together) by reminding his readers of the nature of his gospel.

"But I certify you" should read, "For I make known to you" (v. 11). *The Twentieth Century New Testament* reads "I would remind you." Paul refers back to the "gospel which was preached [literally, gospelized] by me." Note the play on the word *gospel*. The phrase may also be translated "the evangel which was evangelized by me." It was/is not "after" or "according to man." It had no human origin. But Paul's primary thought here is not so much *origin* as *nature*. Verse 12 deals with the former idea. The quality of the gospel which he preached did not correspond to human standards or current ideas. This is a direct slap at the Judaizers whose teachings were according to Jewish tradition.

The "I" in verse 12 is emphatic. It sets Paul's concept of himself over against the picture of him as presented by the Judaizers. He did not receive his gospel from any man. Neither was he taught it by a man. "But" it came to him "through a revelation of Jesus Christ" (RSV). *But* is adversative, setting this method over against the false claims of the Judaizers. The revelation should not be construed as just one revelation. Certainly Jesus revealed himself to Paul on the Damascus road as the living Christ (Acts 9:5), and also in Arabia (Gal. 1:17). In 2 Corinthians 12:1 Paul speaks of visions and revelations, and goes on in verses 2–4 to relate anonymously what is regarded as his own experience. Verse 12 does not mean that Paul received no information about Jesus' life and ministry from any of those who were associated with him (1 Cor. 15:3–7). The primary emphasis is upon the contents of the gospel and Paul's interpretation of it. This would explain his great emphasis upon salvation by grace through faith in Jesus.

In verses 13–14 Paul shows that if men had been choosing an apostle, he probably would have been the last one they would have chosen. His readers were aware of his former manner of life in Judaism. *Conversation* translates a word meaning a going back and forth. In Ephesians 2:3 Paul used the verb form to express the Jewish way of life. Of the Gentiles' manner of life he used another verb meaning walking around (Eph. 2:2). But the sense of both is the same. The word *conversation* is not a bad translation. *We talk as we walk.* And Paul's *talk* prior to his becoming a Christian certainly did not recommend him to an apostleship.

"Beyond measure I persecuted the church of God, and wasted it" (v. 13). *Beyond measure* translates a phrase which means literally "according to a casting beyond" or "in excess." Note that he persecuted the church *of God* (cf. Acts 20:28). He *wasted it.* This is the same verb used by the Christians in Damascus about Paul while he was still Saul of Tarsus (Acts 9:21). A. T. Robertson comments, "Paul heard them use it of him and it stuck in his mind" (p. 278). Various translations render it "did my best to destroy it" (Phillips); "made havoc of it" (Weymouth); "strove to root it out" (Conybeare). His ambition was to destroy the Christian movement, and to erase from the earth the name of Jesus whom he considered an imposter and the enemy of all that he held dear in religion. Because of this fanatical zeal he had risen above his young contemporaries in Judaism (v. 14).

And then the change came! But Paul does not date it from his Damascus road experience (v. 15). To be sure that was the point in history when God's good pleasure was made evident. But Paul sees God's purpose for him even before his birth. This places him definitely in the prophetic tradition (Isa. 49:1, 5; Jer. 1:5). God had a purpose for Paul, even as he has one for each of us. But, like Paul, we must respond to his call. It was through no merit on Paul's part which prompted God to choose him. Certainly it was not through legalism, since he was an unborn child. Rather God called him through [*dia*] his grace or his unmerited favor bestowed upon this unborn child. He did so through his sovereign will, which means that he did it without the advice or consent of anyone outside himself. Of course, Paul was not a puppet but a person who was free to accept or reject God's call.

Verse 16a continues the thought of the previous

verse. God's purpose was "to reveal his Son in me." Lightfoot sees "in me" to mean "through me." However, had this been Paul's idea it seems that he would have used *dia* (through) rather than *en* (in the sphere of). MacGorman sees this as "a definition of conversion: God's revelation of Jesus Christ, his Son, in us! Nothing less than this is enough; nothing more is possible" (p. 87). This seems to capture Paul's meaning (1 Cor. 15:10).

But God revealed his Son in Paul in order that he might preach the gospel among the *heathen,* or Gentiles. Phillips translates the word "non-Jewish world." This points to the problem of Gentile salvation. The Lord had told Ananias that "he [Paul] is a chosen vessel unto me, to bear my name before the Gentiles" (Acts 9:15). Here *Gentiles* translates the same word rendered *heathen* in verse 16. The Judaizers were disturbing the very people to whom Paul was to minister. They had invaded his realm of responsibility with their Jewish legalism. In his missionary work Paul did not ignore Jews (Rom. 1:16). His policy was always "to the Jew first." But when as a group they opposed the gospel he always turned to the Gentiles, his primary responsibility (Acts 13:45–46; 18:6; 28:23–28).

Following his conversion Paul did not return immediately to Jerusalem (v. 17). He did not at that time confer with the apostles, literally "the before me apostles." While insisting upon his apostleship, he recognizes that the others preceded him in that office. However, two very important things are inferred: (1) he was neither appointed by them nor was he subseryient to them; (2) he did not receive his gospel from them. Instead, he went into Arabia, and after that returned to Damascus.

What does Paul mean by *Arabia?* This term may apply to the desert region east of Damascus which extends southward into the Sinai peninsula. Some interpreters see Paul as going to Mt. Sinai where Moses had received the law. If so, it is difficult to understand why after this he would return so far northward to Damascus. It seems more likely that he went into the desert near Damascus.

Why did he go into the desert? In verse 16 he says that "immediately I conferred not with flesh and blood." His emphasis is upon how and from whom he received his gospel. Like Moses, Elijah, and, even Jesus, he needed to spend time alone with God before beginning his ministry. When he learned that Jesus was truly alive, contrary to the lies of his Jewish superiors (Matt. 28:11–15), his life was completely turned around. He needed to get his bearings both personally and theologically. His experience recorded in 2 Corinthians 12:2–4 may well have taken place during this time.

How long he remained in the desert Paul does not say. But he finally returned to Damascus. Luke in Acts makes no mention of this sojourn in the desert, even though most likely he knew about it. This may be explained by the fact that this was such a deeply personal experience that even when he referred to it (2 Cor. 12:2–4), Paul did so in the third person.

Robertson places this desert visit between verses 22 and 23 of Acts 9.

A casual reading of Luke's account could lead us to see Paul returning to Jerusalem after a relatively short period. But the "many days" of Acts 9:23 ("considerable days," Robertson; "as the days mounted up," NEB) may cover a longer period of indefinite time. However one reads it, Paul's point is clear. He received his apostleship and message from God, not from men.

First Visit to Jerusalem (1:18–22)

After three years Paul returned to Jerusalem (v. 18). This is probably to be dated from the time of his conversion. He left Jerusalem a persecuting rabbi; he returned to Jerusalem a persecuted apostle (Acts 9:1–2, 23–25). Certainly Paul is "Exhibit A" as to the changing power of God's grace!

This time period hardly suggests that he was dependent upon the apostles in Jerusalem for a course of action. Depending upon how long he remained in Arabia, we may say that he had been preaching the gospel for the greater part of three years before he paid his visit of fifteen days to Peter. The best Greek texts here read "Cephas," which is the Aramaic form of *Peter*. The tone of this is that he visited with Peter not as an underling but as an equal.

"But other of the apostles saw I none, save James the Lord's brother" (v. 19). James, Jesus' half-brother, was not one of the original Twelve. He had not been a believer during Jesus' earthly ministry, but he had seen Jesus following his resurrection (Acts 1:22; 1 Cor. 15:7). As the leader of the church in Jerusalem (Acts 15:13), he could in that sense be regarded as an apostle. Paul does not go into the details of this visit as does Luke in Acts 9:26–30a. Since he did not see the other apostles, they probably were not in Jerusalem at the time. So important does Paul regard this matter that he takes a solemn oath before God that he is not falsifying his report (v. 20). In the Greek text, *not* is emphatic.

From Jerusalem Paul went "into the regions of Syria and Cilicia" (v. 21). This agrees with Acts 9:30. He did not return to Judea until some years later (v. 22). All that the churches of this area knew about him was that the former persecutor of the churches was now preaching the gospel of Christ. And they praised God for this fact (vv. 23–24).

This shows that Paul was not idle during the interval before Barnabas brought him to Antioch (Acts 11:25–26). "Seek" and "found" in these verses imply that Paul was not sitting at home in Tarsus. He probably was somewhere in the area preaching the gospel which he had received from the Lord while in the Arabian desert.

However, Paul's point is his complete independence from the other apostles and the church in Jerusalem. And he has made his point.

2

The Gospel in Crisis

Galatians 2

THE GOSPEL always exists in an atmosphere of crisis. Its tension in relationship to the world is within itself a crisis. This is to be expected, since the gospel is a judgment against the world system which refuses to recognize God, his judgment upon sin, and his redemptive purpose for all men.

The greatest danger to the gospel is not opposition from without the Christian ranks. Rather it is the dissension within the Christian fellowship (Acts 20:29–30). This is the danger with which Paul is coping in Galatians. We have seen that the gospel of grace and the validity of Paul's apostleship were inseparable. These two elements are evident in Galatians 2.

37

Second Visit to Jerusalem (2:1)

"Then fourteen years after I went up again to Jerusalem with Barnabas, and took Titus with me also" (v. 1).

Paul has established the fact that the apostles played no part in his conversion. Also that in his first visit to Jerusalem he had only a brief contact with two of them. Now he is beginning to show that the apostles and church in Jerusalem actually accepted him as an apostle with a definite call and assignment from the Lord.

Interpreters differ as to the occasion of this visit. Some see it as the *famine* visit recorded in Acts 11:27–30. However, the contents of Galatians 2:2–10 seem to fit better into the visit recorded in Acts 15. This is what is called the Jerusalem Conference visit. It is the first such conference recorded in the annals of Christianity. It had to do with doctrine. Here we see two autonomous churches cooperating in the matter of the purity of the gospel. True to his purpose, Paul also relates it to the nature of his apostleship which was involved in the question of the gospel as preached by him and Barnabas among the Gentiles. Assuming that the visit in Galatians 2 corresponds with Acts 15, it therefore came shortly after the missionary journey of Paul and Barnabas to South Galatia recorded in Acts 13–14. The date would be about A.D. 49.[1] It is understandable why Paul in this

---

1. See Floyd Hamilton, pp. 18–21 for a discussion of the problem of this visit.

letter would make no mention of the *famine* visit. It had no relationship to the problem with which he is dealing.

The Judaizers came out of the church in Jerusalem (Acts 15:1). Their false teachings affected the church in Antioch. So the two involved churches composed the conference, and the church in Antioch sent a group of its people, including Paul and Barnabas (Acts 15:2) to Jerusalem. There they conferred with the apostles and elders of the Jerusalem church. An analysis of the account in Acts 15 shows three phases of the conference: a general meeting which probably involved all the people of the Jerusalem church, or at least some of them (vv. 4–5); a smaller private meeting of a committee (vv. 6–11); a second general meeting of the church (vv. 12–29).

The Jerusalem Conference decided the issue of Gentile salvation in favor of Paul and Barnabas (Acts 15:13–19). However, this did not end the matter. When the Judaizers lost out on doctrinal grounds, they continued to attack Paul's character and motives.

Those who hold that the visit recorded in Galatians 2 is the *famine* visit claim that in Acts 15:20 Paul made concessions to the Judaizers—something which is not reflected in the tone of Galatians 2. But it should be noted that the things mentioned in Acts 15 are not related to Gentile salvation. They involve both Christian morality and the Gentiles' refraining from customs which would offend their Jewish brethren.

Do the "fourteen years" of Galatians 2:1 date from the time of Paul's conversion or from the time of his return to Jerusalem (1:18)? Both positions have their champions. The dating process of this phase of Paul's ministry is uncertain. Unfortunately, we do not know the exact date of his conversion. It certainly happened sometime between the years 31 and 36. It has been customary by many to place it late in this period. One focal point relating to the date is the reign of Aretas over Damascus (2 Cor. 11:32). Studies now being made in Pauline chronology and not yet published point to a date which would place Paul's conversion early in the period, possibly as early as A.D. 31–32. Therefore, assuming an early date, the fourteen years probably should be dated from Paul's Jerusalem visit of 1:18.

If Paul was converted as early as A.D. 32, then his first visit to Jerusalem would have been in A.D. 35. Fourteen years later would be A.D. 49 which is the usually accepted date for the Jerusalem Conference. Therefore, Galatians 2:1–10 may be seen as Paul's account of the *committee* meeting which was held between the two public meetings.

The Jerusalem Conference (2:2–10)

Paul is careful to show that he was not required by the Jerusalem church or its leaders to appear before them. "I went up by revelation" (v. 2). Though he and his group, including Barnabas and Titus (v. 1), traveled southward, he says that they "went up" to Jerusalem. Since that city was located in the mountains, this was the usual term used for going to Jerusalem (John 7:10, 14).

So vital was the issue involving the purity of the gospel that the Holy Spirit revealed to Paul that he should face the problem at its source. The Judaizers, while not representing the thought of the Jerusalem church, had come from its fellowship. In a sense, he must beard the lion in his den. Those who insist that this was the *famine* visit see the revelation as coming through the prophet Agabus (Acts 11:28). However, this position does not fit into Pauline chronology. Since the pronoun *I* is used in connection with the revelation, it evidently was given directly to Paul who conveyed its message to the church in Antioch.

So they went up to Jerusalem and "communicated that gospel" which he proclaimed to the Gentiles. *Communicated* means that he laid before the church this gospel, the specific gospel he was preaching. *Preach (kērussō)* means to proclaim. The Greek verb was used of a king's herald proclaiming his message to his subjects, who were to hear and heed it as though the king spoke in person. Paul was proclaiming the message of his King. Note that he laid out his gospel "privately" to a selected group "of reputation" or "of repute" (RSV). In Galatians 2:9 Paul names three of these (James, Cephas or Peter, and John). This corresponds to Acts 15:4 where Luke speaks of "apostles and elders." It is natural that this private group would include the leaders of the Jerusalem church.

Four times in this chapter Paul uses the Greek word translated *reputation* or *repute*. It comes from the verb *dokeō,* which has the root meaning of think, believe, suppose, seem. Some see Paul's use of it as irony, as he speaks disparagingly of the Jerusalem leadership in his insistence that he is their equal. Others see it as a term used against Paul by the Judaizers, and which he adopts without irony for his own.[2] The latter position could be true. However, we need not look beneath the surface to see a hidden meaning. Paul's problem was not with the leadership. He had no reason to do other than respect them.

Paul's purpose was to clear up this matter "lest . . . I should run, or had run, in vain." He uses the subjunctive and indicative forms of the same verb—lest in vain or to no purpose he might run in the future or had done so in the past. The entire cause of Gentile missions was in the balance.

While Paul touches upon Luke's account, he primarily gives details not included in Acts. Luke was recording the history of the conference. But Paul was arguing one specific point: the gospel of salvation by grace which involved the nature of his apostleship.

The point at issue centered in the need to circumcise Gentiles. The Jerusalem brethren did not require that Titus be circumcised (Gal. 2:3). In Acts 16:3, Luke relates that Paul had circumcised Timothy who was a half-Jew. He did this to avoid any possible complications with Jews among whom they might minister. But Titus was a full Greek. So neither did the church leadership require his circumcision nor did Paul give in to the demands of the Judaizers for it

---

2. See Gerhard Kittel on *dokeō: Theological Dictionary of the New Testament* (Grand Rapids: Eerdmans, 1964), 2:233.

(Gal. 2:4–5). Strangely some interpreters see in verse 3 that Paul did circumcise Titus for the sake of peace. This position is totally unwarranted in the light of the context.

In verses 4–5 Paul explains the crisis mentioned in verse 3. He refers to "false brethren" (2 Cor. 11: 20)—the Judaizers who posed as Christians but who were really Pharisees. The Greek word is *pseudadelphrous* or *pseudo* brethren. They were not real brethren or Christians. This clarifies Paul's *anathema* in 1:9. These people were not a part of the committee; neither had they been invited to the meeting. They slipped into the meeting to spy on the proceedings. The Greek verb means to spy or to make a treacherous investigation. They sought for ammunition to use against Paul and other of their opponents.

The purpose of this spying was to destroy the freedom which Christians have in Christ Jesus. Note that while the primary issue was Gentile freedom, in using "we" and "us" Paul includes the freedom of all who believe in Christ Jesus. The purpose of the Judaizers was to place Christians in complete bondage as slaves to legalism. The verb translated *bring into bondage* is a compound word—the basic verb meaning "to make a slave" with the prefix *kata* or down—so, to enslave completely. Paul will return to this idea of law in verse 16.

The issue of *Gentile* salvation is not a problem today. But the plural pronouns which denote both Jews and Gentiles bring the problem into the present age. Paul was fighting for a free gospel for all time. Thus his opposition to the Judaizers extends to all who would destroy grace by adding legalism to the plan of salvation.

Paul did not give place or yield to the efforts to place him and others in "subjection" (v. 5). The verb rendered *gave place* is found only here in the New Testament. *Subjection* translates a military term meaning a lining up of soldiers in order under a commander. Paul did not "goose step" to the tune of the false brethren. He persisted in order that the truth of the gospel—salvation by grace through faith—"might continue with you." The verb translated *might continue* could be rendered "might abide through." (It is the verb for abide or remain with the prefix *dia*, through, which intensifies the basic verb). Thus we see that the true gospel was at stake in this confrontation.

"No, not for an hour" poses a problem in interpretation. Some manuscripts do not have the phrase *hois oude* ("to whom not even"). This reading would mean that Paul *did* give in regarding Titus's circumcision "for an hour" or for the sake of harmony. However, this reading is contrary to the entire tone of the epistle. The stronger manuscripts support the reading as found in the King James Version. The Revised Standard Version reads, "To them we did not yield submission even for a moment, that the truth of the gospel might be preserved for you." *The Twentieth Century New Testament* follows this idea—"that the truth of the Good News might be yours always!" Phillips reads that Paul did not give them an "inch, for the gospel for you and all gentiles was at stake."

In verse 6 we have the second and third uses of the word for repute or reputation. Paul starts out to make a statement about the ones "who seemed to be somewhat." Then by way of parenthesis he adds that whatever they were did not matter to him. Because God "accepteth no man's person"—literally, "God does not receive the face of men." God is no respecter of persons—he does not judge a person by his face (note that racial characteristics are revealed most in the face, Acts 10:34).

Some interpreters see this as a disparaging remark about the leaders in the Jerusalem church. But the context hardly allows this (see vv. 7–9). However, what it does do is assert Paul's insistence upon his apostleship as being equal to that of the Twelve. In his Son, God chose them, and he also chose Paul. If anything further is seen in this, it is Paul's defense of the Lord himself in his sovereign choice of apostles. He chose no one on the basis of personal merit. It was/is all of grace. Even so, God chooses to deal with us on this basis. We have no right to make it otherwise.

Then Paul returned to his original statement. These leaders added nothing new to his message. They did not criticize it, delete from it, or add to it. They heard the Judaizers' accusations and Paul's defense (Gal. 2:4–5; Acts 15:5, 12). Then a decision was handed down in favor of Paul and Barnabas and their gospel. Some interpreters see the church leaders as demanding Titus's circumcision, but later being convinced otherwise by Paul's arguments. However, the reading of the best manuscripts (reflected in KJV, RSV, and others as shown above) shows that this demand came from the Judaizers and was opposed by Paul. The local leaders listened to both sides and then reached a decision, as any good committee should do. This is expressed in "contrariwise" (v. 7).

The word translated *saw* means to see with perception. After all, James and John were among those who approved Peter's preaching of the gospel to Cornelius (Acts 11:1–18). Of course, Cornelius was a godfearer (Acts 10:2). He was studying Judaism with a view of possibly becoming a Jew in religion. But he had not yet made the final move into the Jewish religion. He was an uncircumcised Gentile. The Gentiles of Antioch and Galatia were raw pagans. But Titus was an example of the fact that they could be saved by grace through faith apart from legalism.

So the church leaders recognized two distinct spheres of ministry: Paul to the Gentiles and Peter to the Jews. The verb rendered *committed* is a perfect tense of completeness and may read "entrusted." Nothing has been said thus far in the epistle about Peter's peculiar role. But there is no reason to question it (see 1 and 2 Peter). Both men had worked mightily in their respective spheres (v. 8).

"And when James, Cephas [Peter], and John, who seemed to be pillars, perceived the grace that was given unto me, they gave to me and Barnabas the right hands of fellowship; that we should go unto the heathen [Gentiles], and they unto the circumcision [Jews]" (v. 9).

Thus Paul records his complete victory over the

Judaizers in the Jerusalem Conference. Of interest is the fact that the Greek text reads *Iakōbos* (Jacob) for James (James 1:1). This, of course, is simply a transliteration of the Hebrew word into Greek. The same reading is found in 1:19.

In verse 9 we find the fourth use of the verb *dokeō* relative to those who seemed to be of repute in the Jerusalem church. They *seemed* to be "pillars." Robertson calls them "Pillar Apostles." They gave Paul and Barnabas "the right hands of fellowship." *Fellowship* means sharing or having all things in common. Someone defined *fellowship* as "two fellows in the same ship." So when these five men shook hands in agreement on their respective roles, they brushed aside the troublemakers as they agreed on a common task in respective areas. As a young lady on a certain television show used to say, "It is bigger than both of us."

This agreement did not mean that each group would not on occasion preach to the other's primary audience, as the record clearly shows they did. Nor does it mean that there were two different *(heteron)* gospels, one for Gentiles and another for Jews (Acts 15:11). It simply means that these strong men recognized God's genuine calling to both groups. They worked together rather than independently or in opposition to each other. John Wesley is reported as saying, "If your heart be as my heart, give me your hand." This was the spirit shown by these true brethren.

During World War II many Southern Baptists migrated to California, which traditionally had been an area where the American (Northern) Baptist Convention worked. These Southern Baptists founded churches to their own liking. In 1944 these churches at their own request were received into the cooperative fellowship of the Southern Baptist Convention. The American Baptists quite naturally regarded this as an invasion of their territory. Friction developed between the two groups in that state. But following the war, people from all over the nation flocked to California. It became the most rapidly growing state in the Union.

In 1963 the Southern Baptist group held two evangelistic conferences in California. The American Baptists cooperated. At the time I was the president of the Southern Baptist Convention. The president of the American Baptist Convention and I were the principal speakers. In the first of these conferences the executive secretary of American Baptists in the Los Angeles area gave the welcoming address. He rehearsed some history of the relationship of the two groups. Then he spoke something like this. "When Southern Baptists first came to California we regarded you as competitors. But the unprecedented influx of people into the state has overwhelmed us. We could never shoulder this load alone. So we see God's hand at work in your coming. Therefore, we welcome you as fellow-laborers in the work of the Lord." This is the attitude of the Jerusalem leaders toward Paul and Barnabas.

To their hand of fellowship the "Pillar Apostles"

added the request that "we should remember the poor" (v. 10). Paul adds that "the same . . . I also was forward to do." He and Barnabas—and their Gentile converts—had already done this in providing famine relief for Christians in Judea (Acts 11:30). Even as Paul wrote Galatians he was in the process of receiving a relief offering from Gentile churches for relief of the poor brethren in Jerusalem (1 Cor. 16:1–3; 2 Cor. 8–9). He was anxious that this offering would be generous, not only to provide relief but also to demonstrate to Jerusalem Christians the genuine nature of the Christian experience among Gentiles (2 Cor. 9:11–14). While Paul vigorously opposed the Judaizers, he constantly sought to weld a bond of fellowship between Gentile and Jewish Christians.

Before leaving this account of the Jerusalem Conference, we should cite a portion of the letter which the conference sent to Gentile churches. It shows that the position of the Judaizers was not that of the church whence they came.

"The apostles and elders and brethren send greeting unto the brethren which are of the Gentiles in Antioch and Syria and Cilicia: Forasmuch as we have heard, that certain which went out from us have troubled you with words, subverting your souls, saying, Ye must be circumcised, and keep the law: to whom we gave no such commandment: It seemed good unto us being assembled with one accord, to send chosen men unto you with our beloved Barnabas and Paul, Men that have hazarded their lives for the name of our Lord Jesus Christ. We have sent therefore Judas and

Silas, who shall also tell you the same things by mouth. For it seemed good to the Holy Ghost [Spirit], and to us, to lay upon you no greater burden than these necessary things" (Acts 15:23–28). (The "things" had nothing to do with salvation. They involved practices which would offend Jewish Christians, and things involved in Christian morality.)

Certain things are worthy of note about this communication. (1) The decision was unanimous (evidently, since they were a part of the problem, the Judaizers were given no part in the decision). The best texts read "The apostles and the elders [pastors], brethren." But verse 22 includes the "whole church." (2) The Gentile readers are called "brethren," a term for Christians. (3) The Judaizers are not called brethren. (4) The Jerusalem church disavowed the teachings of the Judaizers. (5) The church sent two of its own people to authenticate orally the written letter. This could have been done at Paul's request to avoid the charge that he and Barnabas had forged the letter (1 Cor. 16:3). (6) They expressed love for Paul and Barnabas, and commended them for their work. (7) The church recognized the guidance of the Holy Spirit in its decision. Paul could not have asked for any greater victory.

Confrontation in Antioch (2:11–21)

Paul was certainly elated when he returned to Antioch. But it was to be of short duration. For he faced another crisis which involved, not false teachers, but Peter himself. In Jerusalem he faced Peter as an equal and an ally. In Antioch he *faced him down* over matters of conduct and fidelity.

Peter had stood tall during the Jerusalem Conference. He had made a magnificent speech in support of Gentile freedom (Acts 15:7–11). His concluding statement is a classic. "But we believe that through the grace of the Lord Jesus Christ we [Jews] shall be saved, even as they [Gentiles]" (v. 11). The Judaizers said that Gentiles must become Jews in order to be saved. Peter said to the contrary that both Jews and Gentiles are saved the same way—"through the grace of the Lord Jesus." "Christ" is not in the best texts. In the Greek text the above-quoted words are emphatic. They are set in contrast to verse 10 (legalism) by the adversative *but (alla)*.

"But when Peter was come to Antioch, I withstood him to the face, because he was to be blamed" (v. 11). Here is another adversative *but (de)* which contrasts Peter's present conduct with that in Jerusalem. Incidentally this shows that neither Paul nor Peter regarded the latter as a superior apostle. From this incident some interpreters see a continuing conflict between the two. However, there is no evidence to support this idea. In Corinth Paul deliberately used himself and Apollos, not Peter, to enlarge upon the problem there which also involved Peter (1 Cor. 1:12; 3:4–9). And in 2 Peter 3:15–16 Peter spoke of Paul in endearing terms.

However, there is no question about the incident in Antioch. Paul said, literally, "I stood against him face to face." "He was to be blamed" is an effort to trans-

late a very complicated form of the verb meaning to
know against or to find fault with (periphrastic past
perfect passive). Robertson translates it "he stood
condemned" (also RSV). Weymouth catches the sense
of it: "his conduct condemned him." And what was
this conduct?

When Peter came to Antioch he found Jewish and
Gentile Christians eating together (v. 12), and he
joined them. The verb *eat* is in the imperfect tense,
showing that he had done this on a regular basis. The
Mosaic law did not forbid eating with a Gentile. However, Leviticus 11 sets forth dietary laws for Jews, and
these could be threatened by the joint meals. At any
rate, when "certain ones came from James," Peter
"withdrew" from these meals and "separated" himself
from this social communion with Gentile Christians.
These verbs are also imperfect tenses. He began and
continued to do these things.

Some interpreters see these Jews from Jerusalem as
being sent by James to check on this situation. This
hardly fits the picture of James in verse 9 or in Acts
15. This may be Paul's way of saying that they simply
came from the Jerusalem church. It is possible that
they threatened to report this action of Peter to
James. The Jerusalem Conference did not take up the
matter of social life between Gentile and Jewish Christians. And Peter had already been called before the
Jerusalem church for entering the home of Cornelius
(Acts 11:1–18). His present actions were due to his
fear of "the circumcision." This term could refer to

any Jews, even the Jewish Christians of Antioch, but here it probably refers to the Judaizers.

Peter's action was contagious. For the rest of the Jews also "dissembled" with him. The Greek verb is *sunupokrinomai. Sun* means with. The basic verb means to act a part, as an actor in a drama. He pretends to be someone other than himself. The resultant idea is to act as a hypocrite. Note this word in the verb. The noun is *hupokritēs*. So Peter and his fellow Jewish Christians acted together as hypocrites. Even Barnabas joined in their "dissimulation" (*hupokrisei,* hypocrisy). This was the worst cut of all to Paul. The most excoriating words which ever fell from Jesus' lips were uttered against the sin of hypocrisy (Matt. 23).

These Jewish Christians accepted the Gentiles as Christians, but not as social equals. The result was to regard them as second-class Christians. Its modern equivalent would be for white people to admit that some minority groups could be saved, but to refuse to accept them as equals otherwise.

This was a low point in Paul's experience. So long as Christian leaders stood firm, there was hope. But if they deserted, it would be a terrible, if not fatal, blow to Gentile missions. Robertson says, "It was *Paulus contra mundum* [Paul against the world] in the cause of spiritual freedom in Christ" (p. 287). Once again the gospel of freedom was in danger.

Since Peter was the one who started all this, Paul faced him with it publicly (v. 14). "I said unto Peter

['Cephas' in the best texts] before them all, If thou, being a Jew, livest after the manner of Gentiles, and not as do the Jews, why compellest thou the Gentiles to live as do the Jews?" Had Peter been a nobody his act probably would have gone without notice. But being one of the Christian leaders, his example created a defection on the part of others. The devil prefers to use such people as Peter as a tool. This is the primary reason why Paul had to deal with his fellow-apostle. He had to get at the problem at its source. Peter's offense was public; so the confrontation by Paul was also public—"before them all."

As a Jew, Peter lived the way Gentiles did as he ate with them. But his sudden change in conduct implied that Gentiles must become Jews in religion if he was to continue eating with them. So he wanted them "to live as do the Jews." Does this involve accepting Jewish dietary laws? At any rate this introduced again the matter of legalism for the Gentiles. Paul adds that he and Peter were "Jews by nature" or by birth. "Sinners of the Gentiles" was a Jewish term used in referring to Gentiles (v. 15). Paul used it as a figure of speech, not as a derogatory remark. Such would be out of character for the apostle to the Gentiles. In various of his epistles he showed that Jews and Gentiles were equally sinners before God (Rom. 2; Eph. 2:1–7).

As we read this passage, it is difficult to determine if verses 16–21 are a continuation of Paul's words to Peter, or whether Paul is expounding upon the broader meaning of Peter's act. In either case, he deals with the relation of the Jew to law, especially that of Christian Jews. This is seen in the repeated use of "we" and "I." He speaks of Christian Jews in general, but finally comes to his own experience.

In verse 16 Paul lays down the accepted premise among Christian Jews that they are "not justified by the works of the law, but by the faith of Jesus Christ ['Christ Jesus' in the best Greek texts]." *Justified* renders a legal term meaning acquitted or, in the spiritual sense, set right with God. It means that in his sovereign grace God has declared those who believe in Jesus Christ as being justified before him. It is not an arbitrary act on God's part, but is based upon his redemptive work in Christ. *Law* here is without the definite article. So it denotes any system of legalism. In fact, each use of *law* in verses 16–21 is without the article. Of course, in Paul's mind *law* primarily refers to the Mosaic code, but the use here may be extended to include any code of prescribed conduct including one which a person devises for himself. Even Jews were declared righteous through faith in Jesus Christ. "For by [out of, as the source] works of law [legalism] shall no single flesh be declared righteous" (v. 16, literal; see Rom. 3:20).

Verses 17 and 18 have led interpreters to several different positions (MacGorman, p. 94; Hamilton, p. 28). Paul seems to be saying that when Jews seek to be justified by faith in Jesus Christ rather than through legalism, they are the same as Gentiles whom the Jews call sinners. He then anticipates the question, "Is therefore Christ the minister of sin?" Paul quickly rejects such an idea with his favorite "God forbid!"—

literally, "Let it not come into being!" or "Let such an idea die in the process of being born!"

Then the apostle turns definitely to the actions of these Christian Jews. While he speaks in the first person, he apparently has Peter and his fellow-Christian Jews in mind. Literally, "For if things which I destroyed again I build, I prove myself a transgressor." For instance, in living as a Gentile, Peter tore down the law. If he returns to living as a Jew he tears down salvation by grace, which itself is sin as he transgresses truth. You cannot have it both ways. And, of course, if one follows legalism, he is walking into a blind alley which leads to destruction (v. 16).

It is unthinkable that Christian Jews should become enslaved again to law. "For I through the law am dead to the law, that I might live unto God" (v. 19). The first *I* is emphatic. And both uses of law are without the definite article. Paul says that through legalism he died to legalism. This is a paradoxical statement, but it is true. It was the law which made Paul conscious that he was a sinner (Rom. 7:7–11). Also he realized that he could not be declared righteous before God simply by keeping the law. This led him to turn to God through faith in Christ. Thus he was saved by grace. In so doing he died to legalism in order that he might have salvation life *(zōē)* in God (Rom. 7:4, 6).

"I am crucified with Christ: nevertheless I live; yet not I, but Christ liveth in me" (v. 20). Paul emphasizes his identification *with Christ* by putting that phrase first in the sentence: "With Christ I have been crucified." *Crucified* in the Greek is a perfect passive indicative form—Paul declares that he has been completely crucified with Christ. When sin nailed Jesus to the cross, it also nailed Paul to the cross (cf. Rom. 6:8; Gal. 5:24; 6:14; Col. 2:20). When Christ died for sin, Paul (in his subsequent experience with Christ) died *to* sin. Yet though he keeps on living spiritually, it is no longer he who lives but Christ who lives in him. In the Greek text the *I* is emphatic—it is written out as well as being part of the verb. "No longer *I* live." Paul sets his life over against Christ's life in him. He keeps on living in the sphere of *(en)* faith which rests in the Son of God, who loved him and gave himself on his behalf, as his substitute *(huper)*. Paul's personality is completely united with that of Christ. His victorious Christian life is due to the victory of Christ over sin, death, and the grave (Rom. 7:25).

Paul closes this portion of his argument by noting that such an experience does not *frustrate* or make void God's grace (v. 21). Rather it shows the absolute necessity for salvation by grace. If he could have been justified through legalism, then Christ's death would be robbed of all meaning. The Revised Standard Version reads, "Then Christ died to no purpose." Moffatt reads, "I am not annulling God's grace; no, but if saving righteousness comes by way of the Law, then indeed Christ's death was useless."

Therefore, the crisis which Paul faced in confronting the Judaizers—and Peter with the others in Antioch—is more than semantics. It involves the salvation of souls. Even more, it involves the very character of God. If legalism is sufficient for salvation, then God sent his Son on a useless mission of redemption—indeed, he murdered his Son instead of giving him as a necessary sacrifice for sin.

Those today who teach salvation by works plus faith in Christ should ponder Paul's words; they involve far more than merely a difference in vocabulary.

3

Gospel
versus Law (I)

Galatians 3

UP TO this point in the epistle, Paul has dealt with
the problem of the Judaizers as such. He has success-
fully argued for the genuineness of his apostleship
and the true nature of the gospel. His inside story of
the Jerusalem Conference has shown that both he
and the gospel of grace have been vindicated. Now
he turns to deal with the problem as it has affected the
churches in Galatia. He both scolds and loves, debates
and woos, and refers to their experience and the
scriptures. Through it all he shows what Christ has
done for them, and what is involved if they turn from
freedom in him to the bondage of legalism. Indeed,
he employs every available resource in an effort to
stabilize his readers in their faith. The theme running
throughout chapters 3 and 4 is *the gospel versus the law.*

Argument from Experience (3:1–5)

Since expressing wonder as to the instability of the Galatians in 1:6, Paul has spoken largely about himself and his experiences. Now he returns to addressing his readers about their own experience. That he is both mystified and frustrated over their conduct is evident from the manner in which he addresses them.

"O foolish Galatians, who hath bewitched you, that ye should not obey the truth, before whose eyes Jesus Christ hath been evidently set forth, crucified among you?" (v. 1). Neither "that ye should not obey the truth" (see 5:7) nor "among you" is found in the best Greek texts.

The word rendered *foolish* means without mind or senseless. *The New English Bible* translates it "stupid." Phillips makes it even stronger: "O you dear idiots of Galatia." However, both of these seem to be what MacGorman calls "a bit overripe." But Phillips does soften his rendition by injecting the element of love. The idea seems to be that the Galatians have not thought through to the final consequences of their actual or considered actions.

"Who hath bewitched you?" Robertson sees this as a reference to some one *(tis)* aggressive Judaizer (see 5:7). Of course, this pronoun could be used in the collective sense. The word rendered *bewitched* is related to witchcraft. It means to cast a spell upon someone through the power of the evil eye. Such would cause someone to act contrary to his normal character. Before the Galatians' very eyes Paul had portrayed Jesus Christ as crucified for them. This in itself shows that they could not be saved through legalism. Else why would the Lord pay such a price for their sins?

Set forth translates a verb meaning to write beforehand. It was used of a public proclamation such as a placard or notice posted in a public place. One use in the papyri is that of a father posting a notice that no longer would he be responsible for his son's debts. Such notices were posted in the marketplace or other public places, since there were no newspapers or other means of spreading information. One might even carry about a placard containing his message.

Had Paul carried a placard proclaiming Christ's crucifixion, he would have used this verb. The word translated *crucified* is a perfect passive participle. It expresses the idea that Jesus was crucified by someone else and that it has lasting effect. It is this from which the Galatians are turning.

MacGorman says, "In popular lore one did not come under the power of the evil eye until transfixed by its gaze. Thus if the Galatians had kept their eyes where they belonged, this would never have happened" (p. 96). So long as Peter kept his eyes fixed upon Jesus he walked on the water. It was when he looked down at the boisterous sea that he began to sink (Matt. 14:28–30; see Heb. 12:1–2). The wandering sheep is easy prey for wolves. In aerial warfare planes fly in formation for comparative safety. The plane that leaves the formation becomes a "sitting duck." Christians should ever keep their eyes upon Jesus, the pioneer and goal of our faith.

Because the Galatian Christians had not done this, they were being bewitched. Criswell says, "They had turned from Calvary to Sinai, from sonship to serfdom, from liberty and freedom to bondage, from faith to works, from Christ to ceremonies" (p. 74).

In verses 2–5 Paul asks four rhetorical questions. He does not expect or receive answers to these questions. But in interrogative fashion he sets forth evident facts. These questions are posed in the light of the contrast found in verse 1: God's redemptive work in Christ by way of the cross, and the legalism offered by the bewitching Judaizers.

"This only would I learn of you" (v. 2). Then he asks the first question. "Received ye the Spirit by [out of] the works of the law, or by the hearing of faith?" *Law* is without the definite article—so any form of legalism, though Paul has in mind the Mosaic law. Is the law the source whence came the Holy Spirit to indwell them when they became Christians? Or was it the "out of the hearing of faith?" In this sense Paul is talking about the kind of hearing of the gospel which led to faith in Christ (John 14:17; Acts 10:44; Rom. 8:9; Eph. 1:13b–14).

"Are ye so foolish? having begun in the Spirit, are ye now made perfect by the flesh?" (v. 3). The answer to the first question is found in the second one. Assuming that they received the Holy Spirit through faith in Christ, how do the Galatians propose to reach maturity in their Christian experience? They began in the Spirit. Will they now rely upon the flesh? Note the change from faith-hearing to Spirit. Also from faith to works or "flesh." *Flesh* refers to circumcision plus that which they did for themselves by keeping the Mosaic law. This is seen in the middle voice of *made perfect,* a verb meaning to reach an intended goal. Reaching the goal of maturity is the work of the Spirit, not of a person's own will power by law.

The Holy Spirit not only effects regeneration (John 3:5) and seals the saved as God's own (Eph. 1:13b), he also works in believers to develop them from babes in Christ into adults in him (1 Cor. 3:1). In fact, *perfect* may well be translated *adult* or *maturity* (Eph. 4:13b). The Judaizers proposed that after circumcision and faith in Christ, growth in the Christian life came through legalism. So Paul asks if having begun in the Spirit, do they propose to reach maturity through the law? One can hear the irony in his voice as he asked this question. Consistency was a rare jewel indeed among these Galatians.

However, their attitude is not confined to the first century. Among so many Christians today the emphasis in their lives is upon *doing* rather than *becoming.* They are concerned not with what they are doing for Christ, but with what they are *not* doing in the area of personal conduct. To them a good Christian is one who refrains from doing wrong. By this standard, any clothing-store dummy is better qualified as *good.* The emphasis should be upon what we are doing for God and man that is worthwhile. It is possible to be good, but good-for-nothing.

The third question relates to the experience of the Galatians since becoming Christians. "Have ye suffered so many things in vain? if it be yet in vain" (v. 4). The verb rendered *suffered (paschō)* may refer to either a good or a painful experience. *The New English Bible* treats it in the good sense. "'Have all your great experiences been in vain?—if vain indeed they should be." Weymouth is neutral, but could be read in the good sense. However, the sense of suffering came to be the dominant one, and there is no real reason why it should not be seen here. Acts 14:2, 5, 19, 22 shows that persecution did occur in South Galatia. Evidently it had continued since Paul and Barnabas were there. This persecution originated in Jewish opposition. Now these Christians were being asked to become Jews in religion plus having faith in Christ. Have they suffered to no good end?

"If it yet be in vain" suggests that Paul still has hope that the situation in Galatia could be saved. The added phrase was a tactful move on his part to encourage the readers to stand fast. No matter how serious things were, they could still be salvaged.

The apostle's final question (v. 5) relates to the first one about the Spirit in verse 2. Here Paul is referring to God who "ministereth [supplies] to you the Spirit, and worketh miracles among you." The word translated *worketh (energōn)* is brought over into English as *energy.* "Among you" may better read "in you," but either makes sense. The question comes at the end of the verse. Does God supply the Spirit to the Galatians "by works of the law, or by the hearing of faith?" *Law* again does not have the definite article, and can therefore mean the Mosaic law or any legal code. The answer to the question is obvious—the Spirit comes by hearing and obedience of faith.

The accumulative effect of these questions is a victory for salvation by grace through faith. Since up to this point legalism had played no part in the Galatians' experience, a fifth question is implied. Why should the Galatians now turn from grace through faith to works plus faith? Paul wrote to the Romans that the Christian experience is one "from faith to faith" (1:17)—a matter of faith from beginning to end—and all by God's grace.

Argument from Scripture (3:6–18)

Having dealt with the problem in Galatia from the standpoint of their experience in Christ, Paul now turns to an argument from the scriptures. He strikes a masterful blow against the Judaizers as he centers his argument in Abraham (cf. Rom. 4). Abraham was the genetical father of the Jewish people. So an illustration drawn from his life would carry great weight.

Not only were the Galatian Gentiles saved by faith, but Abraham was also. "Even as Abraham believed God, and it was accounted to him for righteousness" (v. 6). This is a reference to Genesis 15:6. Despite his and Sarah's advanced ages, he believed God's promise to give him an heir in Isaac (Rom. 4:16–25). Despite the biological problem involved—which at the human level was an impossibility—Abraham believed God's promise to do the *impossible*. In our own case, looking at our sins we say it is impossible for us to be saved. But God has promised to save all who believe in his Son. Thus believing, like Abraham, we believe that God can/will do the *impossibility*.

The Greek word rendered *accounted* is a bookkeeping term. It means to enter into the ledger or to put down to one's account or credit. When Abraham believed God, his faith was entered into his page in God's ledger as righteousness—a state of being justified before God. In a sense across the page of the record of Abraham's sins God wrote the word *righteousness*.

The Bible presents *righteousness* in three ways: that which God is in his nature; that which he requires in man but which man cannot/does not achieve by his own efforts; that which God bestows upon man by grace through faith in Christ. It is this last sense which applies here (Rom. 1:16–17; 10:4). The Judaizers taught righteousness by law plus faith—in other words men must *achieve* rather than *receive* God's righteousness. In 2:16 Paul has shown the impossibility of being declared righteous through law (Rom. 3:20; 10:1–3). God has revealed his bestowed righteousness in Christ (Rom. 3:21–26).

The Greek word translated *righteousness (dikaiosunē)* belongs to a family of nouns ending with the Greek letter *ēta (ē)*. They state something which is not necessarily true, but which is regarded as being true. Thus this word does not mean that a Christian is righteous or sinless, but that in Christ God chooses to regard him as such. It is the God-kind-of-righteousness; not man's achieved righteousness but the righteousness in Christ which God graciously gives to all believers. Someone has described it as being not an attribute but an activity of God wherein in Christ he lifts us out of the wrong and puts us down in the right as though we had never been in the wrong. And it is by grace through faith, not by legalism plus faith.

Jews and Judaizers claimed special privilege in God's economy because they were Abraham's children by birth (Matt. 3:9). The Jews even claimed that Abraham performed more good works than were necessary for his salvation, and that they could draw upon his surplus for their salvation. But in Romans, a companion book to Galatians, Paul has already shown that Abraham himself was declared righteous by faith rather than by works (4:1–5). Thus he reminds his readers that Abraham's true children are such by their faith, not by their works (v. 7).

To the scripture quoted in verse 6 Paul now adds others to support his position. God's redemptive purpose includes Gentiles as well as Jews (v. 8). Paul calls God's promise to Abraham—"In thee shall all nations be blessed"—a gospel before the gospel (Gen. 12:3; 18:18). Thus those who are "the ones out of faith are blessed with faithful Abraham" (v. 9, literal). Furthermore, whosoever seeks to be saved by law dwells under the curse. "For it has been written and stands written [perfect tense, still in force], Cursed is every one who does not continue in every single thing, the things written in the book of the law to do them" (v. 10, literal, quoting Deut. 27:26). This means that if one proposes to be saved by the law he must keep every part of it all the time. It is precisely because of our failure at this point that salvation must be by grace through faith in Christ (James 2:10–11).

That no one is declared righteous before God by merely keeping the law is evident in Habakkuk 2:4. "The just shall live by faith" (v. 11; Rom. 1:17; Heb. 10:38). But the Mosaic law is grounded in works, not in faith. For "the one doing them shall live in them" (v. 12, literal, quoting Lev. 18:5). But "Christ hath redeemed us from the curse of the law" (v. 13). He became a curse in our stead as he died on the cross, because "cursed is every one that hangeth on a tree." This is a reference to Deuteronomy 21:23.

The thought in verses 13–14 is related to verse 10. The common factor is *curse*. Since the curse is related to the law, some interpreters regard verse 13 as involving only Jews and Jewish proselytes. However, since Gentile Christians were being lured toward reliance upon law, they also seem to be involved. This ties in with the thought expressed in verse 14. Christ's redemptive death extends the blessing of Abraham to Gentiles also. It is thus that Gentile believers receive "the promise of the Spirit through faith."

Paul began his argument from scripture with a reference to Abraham. Now in concluding it he returns to him. His thought at this time is a contrast between God's covenant with Abraham and the Mosaic covenant. As we shall see presently, the former was one of grace; the latter was one of law. These correspond to the gospel preached by Paul and the teachings of the Judaizers.

Paul begins by noting that he is speaking "after the manner of men" (v. 15)—he is about to use a "human example" (RSV) to illustrate his point. Thus he argues from the lesser (human) to the greater (divine). The illustration has to do with a human *covenant*. The Greek word so translated was used of both a covenant (contract) and a will (Matt. 26:28; Heb. 9:16–17). It is also used of a testament *(diathēkē, note "New Testament")*. Interpreters differ as to whether Paul here means a *covenant* or a *will. The New English Bible* translates it as "will and testament." Weymouth renders it "covenant," and Williams translates it as "contract." The context here seems to call for "covenant" which was at the human level a contract.

The word translated *confirmed* means to ratify. In the perfect tense, as here, it expresses the idea of completion. When a contract has been fully ratified it cannot be "disannulled" or set aside except by the consent of both parties involved. The present middle (reflexive) form of the verb *addeth* means that one party on his own cannot continue to add items to the original contract.

In verse 16 Paul alludes to the covenant which God made with Abraham. While he speaks of it in terms of "promises made," these promises grew out of the basic covenant recorded in Genesis 12:1–3. The promises concerned Abraham's *seed* and the *land of*

Canaan (Gen. 12:7; 13:15; 17:7; 22:18; 24:7). But before looking at the promises we should examine the basic covenant with Abraham and the Mosaic covenant (Exod. 19:1–6) to which Paul refers in verse 17.

The latter was a conditional covenant of law which involved Israel's role as a priest-nation to the pagan world. It rested upon conditions which must be met by the lesser party, Israel, before it was binding upon the greater party, Jehovah. Note "if" and "then" in Exodus 19:5–6. It was sealed in animal blood (Exod. 24).

The covenant with Abraham, on the other hand, was an unconditional covenant of grace which related to God's redemptive purpose. The covenant concerning the land of Canaan, which grew out of the basic covenant in Genesis 12:1–3, was sealed in animal blood (Gen. 15:7–11). But note that this happened after Abraham "believed in the Lord; and he counted it to him for righteousness" (Gen. 15:6). However, there is no mention in Genesis of the sealing of the basic covenant. The author of Hebrews sees it as being sealed in the blood of Christ (9:11–28).

Thus in this passage (Gal. 3:15–18) Paul is thinking of the covenant of grace made with and through Abraham, and the one made with Israel through Moses. Therefore, we see the contrast between grace and law—the matters involved in the problem in Galatia.

"Now to Abraham and his seed were the promises made" (v. 16). Keep in mind that the promises grew out of the covenant of Genesis 12:1–3. It was/is through Abraham's seed that God's blessing would be extended to all people. Paul points out that *seed* is singular. In 3:29 he notes the collective sense of *seed,* but he relates it there to those who are in Christ. In verse 16 he uses what Robertson calls "a rabbinical refinement" by which he shows that the seed is Christ. "He saith not, And to seeds, as of many; but as of one, And to thy seed, which is Christ." So the promises made to Abraham regarding his seed are fulfilled in Christ. The *blessing* above all others is through Christ. Abraham's seed which defy his ability to count them are those who are in Christ (Gen. 13:16; 17:7; 22:17; 1 Pet. 2:1–10; Rev. 5:9; 7:9).

And now, having shown that the promises made to Abraham are fulfilled in Christ, Paul returns to his original idea that a covenant once ratified cannot be broken (v. 17). The grace covenant of redemption made with Abraham antedated the Mosaic covenant of law and works by "four hundred and thirty years." This is the duration for the sojourn of Israel in Egypt (Exod. 12:40). Genesis 15:13 reads "four hundred years" (Acts 7:6). The Septuagint (Greek translation of the Old Testament) adds words which make this period to include the time when the patriarchs entered Canaan (Gen. 11:31). It should be noted, however, that the promises to Abraham were repeated to Jacob whose family began the Egyptian sojourn.

Some scholars date the exodus of Israel from Egypt in the thirteenth century B.C., while others date it in the fifteenth century. I follow the early date. The Mosaic covenant and law were given approximately three months after Israel left Egypt (Exod. 19 ff.). However one figures this period of time, it does not affect Paul's argument. In fact, the longer the period the stronger becomes Paul's point. He is showing that the covenant of promise which was fulfilled in Christ came more than four centuries before the covenant of law. The former covenant was ratified. It involved salvation (blessing) for all nations (Gen. 12:3); this included Gentiles as well as Israelites or Jews. Paul declares that the covenant of law did not set aside or remove God's ratification of his covenant of grace extended to all people. The latter does not render inoperative (the meaning of "make of none effect") the former. Therefore, even though Israel as a people did not keep the Mosaic covenant, the one with Abraham still stands.

Though the Judaizers recognized Jesus as the Christ, they saw God's full and final revelation, not in him, but in the Mosaic law. Thus they insisted that while Gentiles should believe in Christ, they must first be circumcised and live as Jews in keeping the law. But Paul has shown that the covenant of grace toward all people has not been set aside by the law. In Romans 4 he showed Abraham as being declared righteous before the rite of circumcision was given (Gen. 15; 17). In this and Galatians 3:17 he shows that both the promise and demonstration of God's grace antedated the law.

Thus the apostle concludes that Abraham's inheritance is not by law but by grace (v. 18). "God gave it to Abraham by promise." Note that God "gave" it, Abraham did not earn it through legalism. In fact, the verb *gave* renders a Greek verb *(charizomai)* which is related to *grace (charis)*. So actually God *graced* Abraham by promise. Thus, by reference to scripture, Paul shows that God deals with man in redemption through grace, not by law.

Purpose of Law (3:19–29)

Up until this time Paul's treatment of law has been negative. So one may wonder about the divine purpose of the law. Paul himself asks the question. "What then the law?" (v. 19, literal). Or "Why then the law?" (RSV).

The law was "added" following the covenant made with Abraham. The apostle is careful not to make it a part of that covenant. The law itself was not a transgression. It made evident the sin of man. Man was already transgressing God's will, but only when the specific commands were written down as law did the sin become evident (Rom. 7:7–14). In the Romans passage Paul is describing his pre-Christian experience. The law showed him that he was a sinner in need of salvation. I might enter a dangerous intersection without stopping, not knowing that I am doing wrong. But if a stop sign is placed there, then I am made aware of my wrong. If I still enter without stopping, then I am a deliberate lawbreaker. So it is with sin. George S. Duncan says that "men may *sin* in ignorance, but they *transgress* only when they have a recognized standard of what is right, and it was to provide such a standard that the Law was brought in" (p. 112).

But the law had only an interim role. It was added until the coming of Christ or "the seed . . . to whom the promise was made." The Jews regarded the law as being given by angels (Heb. 1:4). Moses was the mediator through whom the law was given to the people (John 1:17a). A *mediator* was one who stood in the middle between two people. In this sense Moses stood between God and Israel.

"Now a mediator is not a mediator of one, but God is one" (v. 20). Robertson notes that there have been over four hundred interpretations of this verse. But the context seems to mean that whereas the law was given through a mediator, God's covenant with Abraham involved no mediator. It was given directly by God himself. Thus the covenant of grace is superior to the covenant of law.

Because of the superior nature of the covenant with Abraham, Paul raises a question (v. 21). Is the law opposed to the promises made to Abraham? He rejects the idea with his familiar "God forbid." If a law could have made men alive again spiritually, then God's righteousness would originate in legalism. The condition in the "if" clause is one determined as unfilled. Paul has already rejected this idea (2:21). Evidently his opponents had raised this question. The apostle himself raised it for the purpose of rejecting it categorically.

"The scripture hath concluded all under sin" (v.

22). If Paul had any particular scripture passage in mind, he did not cite it. This has led some to speculate about various passages. (Note Gal. 3:10 quoting Deut. 27:26, and passages combined as in Rom. 3:9–18). He probably used the word *scripture* in a general way. *All* renders *ta panta*, all things, which is Paul's term for the totality of all things both natural and spiritual (Rom. 8:19–23). The Greek verb translated *hath concluded* means to imprison. Thus the human race as a whole is put in prison or is confined "under sin." The lid of the dungeon has been closed and locked— which shows our utter helplessness when left to our own power through legalism. The imprisonment has taken place in order that the promise of God's gracious salvation "by [out of— *ek*, source] faith of Jesus Christ" may be given to all who believe in him.

The law has also served a benevolent purpose (v. 23). For before faith came we were kept under law, placed under guard, while in prison to the law, so that we would look toward the faith which was about to be revealed in Jesus Christ. *Kept* is an imperfect tense which expresses what Robertson calls "a long progressive imprisonment." Thus the law exercised a moral restraint until the appearance of Christ.

Then Paul illustrates this truth by drawing upon a custom of his day (vv. 24–25). The King James Version reads that "the law was our schoolmaster to bring us unto Christ, that we might be justified by faith" (v. 24). The word rendered *schoolmaster* is *paidagōgos*, literally, "boy-leader." Since there is no comparable custom in our society, it is virtually impossible to translate it—note "custodian" (RSV), "tutor" (Weymouth), and "strict governess" (Phillips). Conybeare does not translate but describes this person's role: "the slave who leads a child to the house of the schoolmaster" (quoted by W. A. Criswell, pp. 111–13).

There were more slaves than free people in the Roman empire. It has been estimated that three out of every five men were slaves. Greek and Roman families with many slaves put one in charge of the children. He was called a *paidagōgos*. He was not the teacher or *didaskalos*. Actually he exercised moral discipline over the child. One scholar points out that he is usually represented on vases as having a stick in his hand (note Phillips's translation given above). But when the child was old enough to begin his formal education, this slave took him to the teacher (*didaskalos*, schoolmaster) who taught him.

Paul likens the law to this slave. It exercised moral restraint and discipline over its adherents. But this was only the beginning phase which looked to the time when people would be led to Christ—"that we might be justified by [out of] faith." While Christ is the Teacher, we should not see our coming to him merely as advanced education. Being justified points to him as the Redeemer. The law taught moral discipline and exercised restraint. Christ saves us from sin or our failure to live by the demands of law.

Once the *paidagōgos* led the child to the teacher, the child was no longer under the slave's authority. He then was entrusted to the service of the teacher (v. 25). Thus Paul continues his analogy by showing that when faith came in the appearing of Christ, we were/ are no longer under the law. We are saved by grace through faith exercised toward Christ. Recently I heard a preacher quote the late C. Roy Angell concerning grace. Angell said that grace means that God gives us not what we *deserve* but what we *need*.

Because of God's grace we "are all the children [sons] of God by [through] faith in Christ Jesus" (v. 26). In the Greek text *all* is emphatic. *Faith* has the definite article. It is a particular faith, that which is "in [in the sphere of—*en*] Christ Jesus." The law does not make us Christians. Because of our failure to live by its demands, it leads us to Christ, who saves us by grace through faith. When we receive him, we become children of God (John 1:12).

"For as many of you as have been baptized into Christ have put on Christ" (v. 27). The word *into* translates the preposition *eis,* which may be variously translated for, into, unto, toward as a goal, because of, as the result of, with respect to. The context must decide in each case. In Matthew 12:41 it is translated "at." The men of Nineveh repented not in order that Jonah might preach but as the result of his preaching.

Of interest is the fact that this verse contains Paul's only reference to baptism in this epistle. It is understandable in a letter which emphasizes faith as opposed to works in salvation, for the act of baptism involves works—that of the baptizer and that of the one submitting to it. The New Testament has two Greek nouns for baptism: *baptismos* and *baptisma*. The former denotes the *act* of baptism, and is never used in the New Testament for Christian baptism. The latter connotes the *meaning* in the act. This word is used for Christian baptism (1 Pet. 3:21), and is not found, except in the New Testament and later Christian writings. Apparently it was coined to express the meaning in the act of baptism.

In this light, how does Paul use the verb *have been baptized?* It is a first aorist passive form, pointing to the time when Paul's readers were baptized (immersed) by another person. If one insists that it refers to baptismal regeneration, this would be in direct conflict with Paul's thesis in the epistle. His insistence is that salvation is by grace through faith apart from anything else. In this light it seems that we should regard baptism as symbolic rather than sacramental. This coincides with the use of *baptisma* as the meaning in the act rather than the act itself.

So the probable meaning of the verb here is "baptized with respect to Christ." This meaning also applies to Romans 6:3 where Paul speaks of being baptized with respect to Christ as being baptized with respect to his death. The idea of death is found here in Galatians 3:27. Baptism symbolizes the death, burial, and resurrection of Jesus Christ—that which he did for our redemption. It also depicts that which he does in the believer. The believer dies to his old life which is buried, and he rises to walk in a new life in Christ (Rom. 6:4). It is in this spiritual experience that the believer is in himself clothed with Christ. The verb translated *put on* means to put on as clothes. The middle (reflexive) voice means that one does it within himself. It is not done to him by someone else.

This experience produces a unity among believers (v. 28). The distinctions which once separated people are done away in Christ: racial—"There is neither Jew nor Greek"; social—"there is neither bond [slave] nor free"; sexual—"there is neither male nor female: for ye are all one in Christ Jesus."

When Paul dictated this tremendous verse, he could well have had in mind a prayer of thanksgiving in the ancient Jewish prayer book which expressed thanks to God that a Jewish man was not born a Gentile, a slave, or a woman. Certainly Paul covered all three of these categories, showing that they were negated by Jesus Christ. There is no racial problem today to compare with that between Jews and Gentiles in the first century. One rabbi said that Gentiles were but fuel for the fires of hell. Gentiles were regarded as being outside the circle of God's love and mercy. This was the heart of the Judaizer problem. Already we have noted the slave-freeman situation. And women were regarded as little more than the property of their husbands. But Christ had brought a new relationship in all three areas.

Later, writing the Ephesian letter, Paul shows God's purpose in Christ concerning Jews and Gentiles. "For to make in himself [Christ] of twain one new man, so making peace" (Eph. 2:15). In Christ God made a new order of mankind—Christians. One Jew plus one Gentile plus Christ equals two Christian brethren.

Use any combination of races, nationalities, or classes, and the answer is the same.[1]

"And if ye be Christ's, then are ye Abraham's seed, and heirs according to the promise" (v. 29).

Paul has shown that one is a child of Abraham through faith rather than through natural birth. The Judaizers taught that Gentiles must become Abraham's children by law before believing in Jesus. Paul has taken the opposite position. Jews must believe in Jesus in order to become Abraham's true seed. Thus both Jews and Gentiles stand on an equal basis before God. The law makes neither a child of Abraham nor a child of God. It only gives moral instruction and provides moral restraint. Sonship and heirship come by grace through faith in Abraham's Seed—Christ.

"If ye be Christ's" implies that this is true of Paul's readers. Commenting on this phrase Robertson says, "This is the test, not the accident of blood, pride of race or nation, habiliments or environment of dress or family, whether man or woman. Thus one comes to belong to the seed of Abraham and to be an heir according to promise" (p. 299).

---

1. See Herschel H. Hobbs, *New Men in Christ* (Waco: Word Books, 1971).

4

Gospel versus Law (II)

Galatians 4

THE BREAK between chapters 3 and 4 does not constitute a break in Paul's thought. In chapter 4 he continues to treat the general theme of the gospel versus law. In fact he continues to show how the law finds its complement in the gospel of grace. The two do not run concurrently but in succession. At the point where the effectiveness of law ends, the gospel takes over and carries our spiritual experience on to completion. It is not possible, therefore, to mix gospel and law as the Judaizers proposed.

Law as a Guardian (4:1–7)

The use of the word *heirs* in 3:29 suggests the further relation of a child to those who are charged with his welfare. This picture also Paul applies to the function of the law. Thus from another human example he illustrates spiritual truth.

In verses 1 and 2 Paul cites four people: heir, father, tutors, governors. The situation assumes that the father is dead. (This should not be seen as teaching that God is dead. No human examples can fully express spiritual truth.) In his will he "appointed" the time when the son would come into full control of his heirship. *Appointed* translates a word that has in it the idea of "beforehand"—the father did the appointing before his death, at the time he made his will. He placed his nonage son under tutors and governors.

Various ancient legal systems provided for such an eventuality. For instance, later Roman law provided for the child to be under a guardian (tutor) appointed by the father, until he was fourteen. Then he was under a governor (steward) appointed by the state, until he was twenty-five. Earlier Graeco-Phrygian cities had a similar law, except that the father appointed both tutor and governor.

However, it is not necessary to see either of these in Paul's example. He is probably using a general case. The point is that the heir did not receive his full inheritance until the authority of these two guardians ended. During that time, he was no different than a slave, even though he actually was "lord of all." *Lord* translates *kurios* which may mean Lord referring to God, lord, sir, or owner. The last meaning applies here.

In the same way, "we, when we were children, were in bondage under the elements of the world" (v. 3).

We is emphatic in the Greek text. The verb form rendered *in bondage* means a state of complete bondage.
Since Paul has been talking about law, we expect him
to say that we have been in bondage to law. But he
uses a phrase which may be translated "the basic elements of the cosmos" or "world."

The word translated *elements (stoicheia)* has several
possible meanings. The basic word *stoichos* means a
row or a series of things. It can mean the basic elements of the universe, the heavenly bodies, or the
rudiments of any act. Some interpreters relate the
idea of being in bondage to the elements to star-
worship among pagans. But since Paul uses the plural
we, he includes both Jews and Gentiles. Robertson
notes that *ta stoicheia* can refer to the beginning of a
series, like the first letters of the alphabet. We would
say the ABCs of something. It is so used in Hebrews
5:12, where it is translated "first principles." Modern
translations vary between these two ideas. For instance, the *New English Bible* reads "the elemental
spirits of the universe." Conybeare says "our child-
hood lessons of outward ordinances." Phillips renders
it "basic moral principles."

Paul's theme of "law" probably means that prior to
Christ's coming, both Jews and Gentiles were in slavery to the ABCs of God's revelation through law. In
Romans 2:11–15 Paul shows that the Jews have God's
written law, and the Gentiles have God's law written
in their hearts. Thus, as they live under legalism, both
are in the ABCs of God's revelation. MacGorman
suggests that "Paul is describing the time under law

for the Jews and the pre-evangelical experience of the Galatians as a period of nonage. It was a time in which they were governed by mere rudiments. It was both temporary and preparatory; it anticipated fulfillment" (p. 106). This corresponds to the time when they were in the ABCs of God's revelation. This state looked forward to God's full revelation in his Son.

Thus those who still rely upon legalism have stayed in the preliminary state of bondage. They have not yet come to know the spiritual freedom in Christ. Many years ago I was invited to preach in a synagogue service. As I heard the people going through their Old Testament rituals, I wanted to cry out, "There is *more!*" This is what Paul is saying to his readers.

In verses 4–7 Paul tells us about this *more.* "And when the fulness of the time was come, God sent forth his Son, made of [out of] a woman, made under the law, to redeem them that were under the law, that we might receive the adoption of sons" (vv. 4–5). *Law* in both verses has no definite article. In verse 4 it refers to the Mosaic law. In verse 5 it should probably be translated *legalism,* including both the Mosaic law and God's law placed in pagan hearts. It could also include any legalistic code of conduct.

Time here means chronological time, historical time. Its "fulness" can refer to the time which seemed right in God's wisdom. Some interpreters see this as the time when Greek culture, Roman law, and Jewish hope came together to produce the condition envisioned by God. However, as Duncan says, "It was not man's *progress* which impelled God to act, but

man's *need*" (p. 128). MacGorman sees it as "the
sovereign decision of a living God, who is mercifully
disposed toward us." But in keeping with the companion teachings of man's free will and God's sover-
eignty, it seems that we must involve both God and
man in the meaning. Furthermore, this statement cannot be read in isolation from Paul's treatment of law.

Someone may ask why, since God knew from the
beginning that man could/would not be saved by law,
he waited so long to send his Son through whom he
offers man salvation by grace through faith? To me
the logical answer is that while God knew it, man did
not. Through trial and failure he had to learn that
legalism could not satisfy the deeper longings of the
soul. Of course, most Jews, including the Judaizers,
held on to law. But man's failure in legalism produced
a spiritual climate in which many would turn from
legalism to Christ. Some Jews did so. But the greater
reception of Christ was among the Gentiles who were
disillusioned with their pagan gods. But however one
may interpret this "fulness of time," it shows that God
took the initiative in meeting man's need. This is always the case. For the Bible teaches that forgiveness
was in God's heart before sin was in man's heart (Eph.
4:3; Rev. 13:8).

Some critics of the virgin birth of Jesus make much
of the fact that neither John's Gospel nor Paul teaches
it. For that matter, neither does Mark, since he begins
his Gospel with the public ministry of John the Baptist
and Jesus. While John does not spell it out as do
Matthew and Luke, he certainly implies it in John

1:14. Among John's purposes in writing was that of supplementing the other Gospels. Since Jesus' virgin birth was already fully treated by Matthew and Luke, he implies it and then goes on to record information which they omit. *But how many times does the Bible need to state something for it to be true?*

As for Paul's account, here he calls Jesus God's Son. The Greek reads literally "the God the Son of him," specifying God's unique Son, "coming into being out of a woman." He *became* what he had not been before—a flesh-and-blood man (John 1:14). Like begets like—a horse a horse, and God God. How else could Jesus be God's unique Son than by the Holy Spirit's conceiving power (Matt. 1:18, 20; Luke 1:35)? In calling Jesus God's Son, Paul points to his deity. His "coming into being out of a woman" speaks of his humanity. Thus he is both God and man—the God-Man. Jesus' humanity is further stressed by his coming into being "under the law" or "under law"—legalism prior to God's offer of grace through him.

The double purpose of the incarnation is seen in verse 5. It was that Christ might redeem those "living under law," literally, "the ones under law." The phrase is in the emphatic position in the Greek text. The verb translated *redeem* is built upon the word for *marketplace (agora)*. The compound verb used here means "to buy out of the marketplace." This implies the price of redemption. It is not a price paid to Satan, else he would be more powerful than God. It was paid to God himself in order to satisfy the demands of his holy, righteous nature. Actually it was to satisfy the demands of God's law under which men were held in bondage. In his sinless life, Jesus fully met the law's demands. He was tempted in all areas, just as we are, yet he was without sin (Heb. 4:15). By meeting the law's demands, he showed God to be *just* in those demands. Then he was made sin on our behalf, that we might be made God's righteousness through faith in him (2 Cor. 5:21). Thus God in Christ became "the *justifier* of him which believeth in Jesus" (Rom. 3:26). Someone has said that the fact that Jesus lived in a flesh-and-blood body, in a corrupt society, and endured every kind of temptation without committing sin, is as great a miracle in the moral sphere as his virgin birth was in the biological sphere.

The other purpose of the incarnation is "that we might receive the adoption of sons." "Of sons" is not in the Greek text, but it is present in the Greek word translated *adoption,* which means the making of a son. In speaking of this same experience, Jesus used the vital picture of "birth from above" (John 3:3). Paul uses the Roman law of adoption. A man might adopt a son, usually a slave. The ceremony included the adopting father paying the price for a slave's release, or, if a free child, assuming all his obligations. The adopted son was said to be born again into a new family with new relationships. He received all the privileges of naturally born sons, including joint-heirship. Also he assumed the responsibilities of sonship. At least two witnesses were required in such a transaction. Here the two witnesses are the Holy Spirit and the believer's heart (v. 6; see Rom. 8:16).

Paul describes this more at length in Romans 8:14–18.

"Because ye are sons [not slaves], God hath sent forth the Spirit of his Son into your hearts, crying, Abba, Father" (v. 6). *Abba* is the Aramaic word for *Father*. The dual use of this idea probably reflects the language of a little child. The result of this experience is that the Gentile believer (note the singular pronoun *thou*) is no longer a slave to law, but is a son of God (v. 7). *"Thou"* singles out each Gentile believer. Each one as a son is God's heir through Christ. Whereas in Romans 8 Paul stresses joint-heirship with Jesus Christ, the point here seems to be joint-heirship with Jewish Christians. God makes no distinction between the two. In Christ each has graduated from nonage to maturity, so that he truly becomes "owner of all" (v. 1).

Warning against Legalism (4:8–11)

Up to this point in Galatians, Paul's greater emphasis has been upon coming out of bondage to legalism into freedom in Christ by God's grace. But having reached a climax in 4:7, he suddenly returns to the present danger in the Galatian churches—a tendency to forsake all this for a relapse into legal slavery. Thus he warns his readers against a return to legalism.

Before the Galatians became Christians, "not knowing God, ye served the ones by nature not being gods" (v. 8, literal). *Served* here means to serve as slaves. A historical aorist tense, it covers the Galatians' entire pre-Christian experience. Whether this service as religious slaves centered in crude idols, ideas, men, or the entire order of Greek gods doesn't matter. These entities are really "no gods"—nothing. In 1 Corinthians 8:4–6 Paul has already declared that such are "gods so-called." Then in 1 Corinthians 10:20 he speaks of pagan sacrifices being sacrifices to demons. The pagan gods are still no-gods. But through these false gods, demons lead their devotees away from the true God. So not only does Paul deny *deity* to these pagan gods, he labels worship of them as demonic, devil-worship. People are inherently religious. They are going to worship. By leading them to the *false*, Satan denies to them the *true*.

This is still one of Satan's most effective tools. To spiritually hungry souls he offers pseudonourishment that fills their spiritual capacity but gives no nourishment. 1 John 4:1 warns against evil spirits. We should recall that there is an evil spirit abroad in the land, as well as the Holy Spirit. We are to discern between the two to determine which is of God. "Isms" almost without number are like clouds without water, food without nourishment, and they ever lurk to snatch off the weak and wandering. We are to judge such by their fruit.

In verse 9 the apostle describes these "isms" most clearly. "But now" sets the readers' present experience over against their pre-Christian one. He reminds them that they "have known"—came to know (ingressive aorist participle)—God. Then quickly he changes his emphasis—they really have come to be known by God. This emphasizes God's initiative in their salvation. In paganism they sought God. In the Christian revelation God sought them. This is the difference between *religion* and *Christianity.*

The force of "but now" continues as Paul asks why, after having known the freedom which God in Christ gives, they are now once again returning to the ABCs of legalism which enslaves them (v. 3, the Greek reads "wish to enslave"). Note that he calls these elements "weak and beggarly." Phillips calls them "dead and sterile." *Beggarly* translates a word which describes abject poverty, reducing one to being a beggar. Instead of being strong and able to contribute to our spiritual needs, these ABCs are weak and beg us to contribute to them. Christ offers to give the abundant or overflowing life (John 10:10), but these elements rob us of even that which we have. As we have seen in 4:3, these ABCs are the legalism into which the Judaizers wish to lead the Galatians.

While circumcision was the heart of the Judaizers' teaching, Paul lists in verse 10 the things which are involved in living by the Mosaic law: days (Sabbaths, fast days, feast days, new moons), months (particularly observed during the Babylonian exile, Isa. 66:23), times or seasons (passover, pentecost, tabernacles, dedication), and years (the sabbatical year every seventh year and the year of Jubilee). Robertson, after listing the above, says, "Paul does not object to these observances for he kept [some of] them himself as a Jew. He objected to Gentiles taking them as a means of salvation" (p. 303).

Paul closes this warning with a sharp expression of

foreboding. "I am afraid of you" (v. 11). Or with respect to you. "Have bestowed labour" is a perfect indicative form of the verb meaning to do toilsome labor. Had he used the subjunctive mode it would express a fear about what might be true in the future. But the perfect indicative form shows that he fears that it is now a fact. *The Twentieth Century New Testament* reads, "You make me fear that the labour which I have spent on you may have been wasted."

Floyd Hamilton says, "Paul was afraid of spiritual disappointment over a possible apostasy of the Galatians, but there is a deeper fear lest they should show by such apostasy that they are not really born again" (p. 44). Alas, how such a fear tugs at the heart of every Christian pastor and teacher who sees how unstable and/or nonproductive are so many with whom he/she has labored.

MacGorman makes a concluding comment which should be pondered by every professing Christian. "The movement from pagan worship to Christian deliverance to Jewish legalism is not faith perfected, as claimed by the Judaizers. It is faith rejected, a reversion to their former enslavement" (p. 108).

Friendly Appeal (4:12–20)

In this passage the tone of Paul's letter suddenly changes from argument and accusation to appeal on the basis of friendship. He reminds his readers of their former relationship.

The Greek text of verse 12 reads literally, "Become as I, because also I as you, brethren, I beseech you."

In spite of all that has happened, Paul still regards them as *brethren* in the Lord. But his emphasis is upon his plea that they become as he is. He still trusts in Christ alone and wants them to do the same. His becoming as they are probably means that he had forsaken Jewish trust in law to trust only in Christ as they have done (1 Cor. 9:21). Though the cause is desperate Paul does not give up.

"Ye have not injured me at all" (v. 12b). Or "You did me no wrong" (RSV). Various views are held as to the apostle's meaning here. Do the Judaizers claim that they did Paul no wrong in preaching what they called a more authentic gospel? Or have the Galatians insisted that they did him no wrong in accepting it? Is this a general disclaimer of any grievance Paul might hold against them? Or does it refer to their treatment of him when he first preached the gospel among them? The simple truth is that we cannot say with certainty. It may involve some occasion unknown to us. The plain truth is that, whatever is involved, Paul holds no grudge against his readers. For this reason they should be able to resolve their difference of opinion. He is not proposing a compromise, but is clearing the air of any misunderstanding on their part.

Verses 12–15 contain a rehearsal of events on his first visit to Galatia. "Ye know how through infirmity of the flesh I preached the gospel unto you at the first" (v. 13). *Know* translates a verb *(oidate)* which means perceptive knowledge. It could read "really know" or "know full well." "At the first" can mean that, or it can read "the former time." *The New English Bible* reads "originally." Phillips has it "when I first."

When was this time when Paul "first" preached the gospel in this area? Of course, *first* suggests that there was also a second time. Those who hold to the North Galatian theory see these two times in Acts 16:6 and 18:23. Those who see the letter as written to churches in South Galatia see the two visits as coming during Paul's first missionary journey (Acts 13:4–14:28). However, it seems more natural to place the first visit during this period, with the second recorded in Acts 15:41–16:6. But however one may figure this, the first visit most likely was during the first missionary journey.

What his infirmity or sickness was, Paul does not say. Some see it as epilepsy! On the basis of Galatians 4:15 and 6:11, others hold to the view of eye trouble. Still others think that it was malaria. Paul and Barnabas landed in Asia Minor at Perga in Pamphylia (Acts 13:13)—an area which was infested with malaria. It is highly possible that Paul contracted malaria there. By the time he reached the highlands he could have been having chills and fever. These seizures would fit his description in Galatians 4:14. But whatever his problem was, it did not affect adversely his ministry in Galatia.

"And my temptation which was in my flesh ye despised not, nor rejected; but received me as an angel of God, even as Christ Jesus" (v. 14).

Temptation may better read "trial" (RSV). According

to the context, the Greek word may have a good or bad meaning. It really means a testing to determine if something (metal) or someone is good or bad, genuine or false. When used of God, it carries the good sense. In Matthew 4:1 "to be tempted" is an infinitive of purpose. God permitted Jesus to be tested so as to determine his faithfulness to the Father's will in his Messianic role (cf. Gen. 22:1). The devil tempted Jesus in an effort to get him to renounce God's will in favor of Satan's will.

However, in Galatians 4:14 the word does not necessarily involve either of these uses. Paul's condition was a physical trial. Some late manuscripts read "my" as in the King James Version. But the oldest reading is "your." Paul's condition was a trial to the Galatians. It was "your trial in my flesh." But despite Paul's physical condition, the Galatians neither "despised" (put themselves away from, shrank from) nor "rejected" him. The Greek word rendered *rejected* means, literally, to spit out, to spurn, or to loathe. Plutarch uses it in the sense of rejection. *The New English Bible* says that they did not "show scorn or disgust."

Instead, the people received Paul as "an angel of God." *Angel* could be translated messenger *(aggelos)*, but in this context *angel* seems to be Paul's meaning. He makes an even stronger statement—they received him "as Christ Jesus." This can hardly refer to his being mistaken at Lystra for Hermes (Mercury), as seen in Acts 14:12–13. Because later, at Jewish instigation, the people turned on him and Barnabas.

Paul's own revulsion at receiving divine worship shows that he does not in any sense equate himself with the Lord. His meaning is that they received him as though Christ Jesus had come in person. They were not attracted by Paul's appearance but by his gospel of salvation for Gentiles—by grace through faith in Jesus Christ.

Paul's experience suggests that we should not rely upon personal charm or ability to draw people to Christ. Salvation comes through their believing the gospel, not through their liking the preacher. If we build about ourselves, the work, like us, will be temporary. Only that which is founded upon Christ abides.

But now the situation has changed. Due to false teaching, the Galatians stand in danger of turning from their former bright hope to be enslaved by legalism. This leads Paul to ask what happened to their "blessedness" or happiness over his presence. The word rendered *blessedness* may also mean a state of having in oneself (in Christ) all that is necessary to live a rich, full life. The Galatians had this through faith in Christ. Now the Judaizers were insisting that obedience to the law is also necessary. They were attacking Paul personally, including his appearance. And the people were easy prey to their tactics. Paul bears personal testimony to the fact that on his first visit, if possible they would have plucked out their own eyes and given them to him. As previously noted, some see this as evidence that Paul had eye trouble. This may be true. But his words seem to be simply a strong statement of the people's loyalty to him (cf. Rom. 16:4). Priscilla and Aquila did not actually stretch out their necks on the executioner's block for Paul; but in some way they did imperil their lives for him.

Certainly the Galatians had regarded Paul as a friend when he gave them the truth of the gospel. But now they were confused by the Judaizers. As Paul repeats this same truth to them, he asks if he has become their enemy (v. 16). Perhaps the Judaizers had accused him of being such. So he puts this in the form of a rhetorical question in order to deny the accusation. We can hardly see the Galatians as calling Paul their enemy. However, he uses the idea to good effect. Of course, he expected a negative answer.

Now Paul plainly repeats the charge that the Judaizers are the cause of the trouble in these churches (v. 17). The words "zealously affect" translate one Greek verb (*zēloō*) which means to have zeal or to burn. In the bad sense, as here, it means to be jealous. The Judaizers had been zealous in teaching their false doctrine. But it was not for the Galatians' good. They wanted to "exclude" them—that is, to shut them out. Some see this to mean exclude from Christ. Others see it as from the gospel of grace. In this context, where Paul is dealing with the Galatians' friendship for him, the more likely thought is that of excluding them from him. Of course, this also involves the gospel which he preached.

If the Judaizers succeeded in their purpose to show that Gentiles must be saved by legalism plus faith in

Christ, the Gentiles would then be separated from Paul and his gospel. The result would be that they would turn to the Judaizers for instruction in the law. The phrase "that ye might affect them" could better be translated "in order that with respect to them you might be zealous." Having shut out Paul, they would have the Galatians to themselves. Thus Paul impugns their selfish motives. He had risked his life to evangelize them. The Judaizers served out of a selfish motive. Here is a striking parallel between Paul's words and Jesus' contrast of false and true shepherds (John 10:10–16). In his interpretative translation, Phillips has caught the sense of Paul's words: "Oh, I know how keen these men are to win you over, but can't you see that it is for their own ends? They would like to see you and me separated altogether, and have your zeal all to themselves."

In verse 18 Paul notes that zeal is good when directed toward a good end. He longs for the Galatians' zeal toward him and the gospel to be as strong in his absence as it was while he was present with them.

Paul closes his appeal to friendship on a tender note (vv. 19–20). "My little children" uses the diminutive form of the word for *children*. They are his spiritual children, since it was through him that they had been born into the family of God. This diminutive form not only adds a tender note, but suggests also that they are still babes in Christ. As once he had endured birth pangs to bring them to Christ, so now he endures the same pains "until Christ be formed in you." This does not mean that they are now lost and must be saved again. The idea is that having become Christians, they should now grow into the likeness of Christ. Hamilton comments, "This is a figure of speech, but it is really true that a Christian is transformed into the image of Christ after his new birth" (p. 46).

Desire (v. 20) is an imperfect tense of the verb to wish. The verse could be translated, "I was wishing and still wish to be [alongside] and face to face with you now." Distance was such a handicap in dealing with this problem. Furthermore, it is impossible to put one's heart and the sound of one's voice into a letter. Writing tends to be a poor substitute for speaking personally. Even though Paul tried to express his love in the words "my little children," that could not fully express in cold, flat paper and ink what was in his heart. At times he wrote harshly to them. If his readers were prone to do so they could take exception to it. But if they could see his eyes and hear the emotion of love in his voice, they would know that what he had said was in love and for their good.

"I stand in doubt of you" may better read, "I am perplexed about you" (RSV). Moffatt reads, "I am at my wits' end about you!" *The Living Bible* says, "For at this distance I frankly don't know what to do."

The verb rendered *stand in doubt* is formed from *poros,* way, with the alpha privative, which negates the main word. In trying to deal with this matter at such a distance, Paul says that he has lost his way. He wanders in a maze. But he tries valiantly to reason with his readers in order to help them in their predicament. If he did not love them, it would not matter. But his is a love which will not let them go—despite the miles which separate them.

Allegorical Example (4:21–31)

Beginning with chapter 3, Paul dealt with the contrast between legalism and freedom in Christ. In 4:12–20 he appealed for loyalty to the gospel of freedom on the basis of mutual friendship between him and the Galatians. Now for the remainder of this chapter he returns to his basic subject. And he does so in a manner which seems strange to modern readers. But the method of *allegory* was an accepted one among rabbis of that time. Using incidents from Genesis (16:1–18:15; 21:1–21), Paul makes an allegorical interpretation in order to show the superiority of the gospel of grace over the legalism which the Judaizers sought to impose on the Galatian Christians.

"Tell me, the ones wishing to be under law [no definite article, so 'legalism'], do you not hear the law?" (v. 21, literal). The portion of "the law" to which Paul refers is not the Mosaic code itself but the passages which the Jews regarded as the *law* (the five books of Moses—Genesis to Deuteronomy). "Hear" carries the idea of understanding what is heard. The word *wishing* (desire) suggests that Paul's readers have not yet made a final decision in the matter.

Verses 22–23 set the scene for Paul's comparison. The Jews emphasized their being descendants of Abraham. Already Paul has shown that the true children of Abraham are those of faith (3:7). Now he takes an even more amazing position in which he uses the figures of Abraham's two sons, Ishmael and Isaac (v. 22). Because Sarah, Abraham's wife, was barren, she gave her handmaiden Hagar to Abraham as a secondary wife, following the custom of the time, as revealed in archaeological records. And Hagar bore Abraham a son, Ishmael. The word Paul uses to describe Hagar is *bondmaid (paidiskēs)*, the female diminutive of *pais*, boy or slave. Hagar was an Egyptian female slave. Several years after Ishmael's birth, in her old age, Sarah gave birth to Isaac, who was the son of God's promise to Abraham. So he was born of a "freewoman."[1] Paul notes that Ishmael was born "after the flesh," or by the normal course of nature. But Isaac was born supranaturally in fulfillment of God's promise (v. 23).

Then Paul proceeds to apply these historical facts to theological truth. "Which things are an allegory" (v. 24). Raymond T. Stamm comments, "When Paul says that these things are 'allegorical utterances,' he

---

1. In modern Israel whether one is a Jew is determined by the mother, not the father. Arabs are descendants of Abraham through Ishmael. Jews are Abraham's descendants through Sarah. They both have the same *father* but different *mothers.* When Abraham and Sarah tried to run ahead of God by trying to get a son through Hagar, they engendered strife which continues to this day. Genesis records the origin not only of the universe and man; but also of one of the most perplexing problems of the modern era—the Israeli-Arab conflict. See Herschel H. Hobbs, *The Original of All Things* (Waco: Word Books, Inc., 1975).

does not mean that the Genesis story is unhistorical myth, but he sees in it a religious meaning that ranges far beyond literal history" (p. 540). Duncan notes, "By an *allegory* he means something more than an *illustration:* it is a spiritual truth embodied in history, a shadow from the eternal world cast upon the sands of time" (p. 144). Stamm further notes that "allegorical interpretation rests upon the belief that every word, figure of speech, and grammatical form in scripture has a special 'spiritual' significance besides its literal meaning." Rabbi Akiba went so far as to find a mystical meaning in every little marking on letters in the Hebrew alphabet. Philo, the Jewish-Alexandrian philosopher-theologian used this method to show that Moses spoke the truth in Greek philosophy long before the Greeks themselves.

Paul does not go to these extremes. But with great skill he uses these figures to make his point. He says, literally, "Which things are allegorized." The Greek verb is *allēgoreō—allo,* "another" and *agoreuō,* "to speak"; in other words, to speak another meaning than what the language openly states. While this verb was used widely among the Greeks, this is its only use in the New Testament.

And what is this allegory? It is that these two women, Hagar and Sarah, stand for two covenants: the one at Sinai and the one made with Abraham (v. 24). Since the Sinai covenant was one of law, it "gendereth to bondage"—"bearing children for slavery" (RSV). Thus it corresponds to Hagar, the slavewoman.

For *Hagar* "is mount Sinai in Arabia, and answereth to Jerusalem which now is, and is in bondage with her children" (v. 25).

There are various Greek manuscript readings on this verse, but the overall sense is that Hagar and her descendants correspond to Mount Sinai with its enslaving law. This further represents the Jerusalem then existing on earth. Thus, like Hagar, all who adhere to the law which centered in Jerusalem (whence come the Judaizers) are still in bondage to legalism. MacGorman is right when he notes that Paul's point is to say that *the Jews are Ishmaelites!* (p. 110). Thus Paul completely turned the Judaizers' argument around. They themselves were spiritual descendants not of Sarah the freewoman but of Hagar the slavewoman! Naturally the Judaizers would reject this. But using a Jewish form of interpretation, Paul established his point with his readers.

"But Jerusalem which is above is free, which is the mother of us all" (v. 26; better reading, "our mother"). Paul does not explain "Jerusalem which is above." He assumed that his readers were aware of its meaning. The symbol had a rich background in both Jewish thought and Christian hope (cf. Ezek. 40–44; Haggai 2:8–9; Zech. 2; Phil. 3:20; Heb. 11:10; 12:22; Rev. 21:2).

Stamm notes that the Jerusalem which now is "was a most unholy 'Holy City,' full of injustice, violence, and murder, and subject [in bondage] to the cruel and wicked rulers imposed by a Gentile empire. But over against this Jerusalem of slavery lay an ideal celestial city, unseen at present, but destined soon to supercede it" (p. 541).

In contrast to Sinai and the earthly Jerusalem which correspond to Hagar, Paul sees the Jerusalem above as corresponding to Sarah and freedom. Her descendants, who are free from law through faith in Christ, her true seed (3:16), are the citizens of this *city*. They are composed of Jews and Gentiles who have been saved by grace through faith in Christ. So whereas the legalistic Jews are really *Ishmaelites*, Christians are the true *Israelites* (Rom. 9:6–7; 1 Pet. 2:1–10). To support his point, Paul quotes Isaiah 54:1 (v. 27). The original reference was to the faithful remnant in Babylonian exile. But Paul applies it to Sarah and her descendants. This is in keeping with the overall teaching of the Bible.

Stamm (p. 539) helps us to see Paul's meaning in a parallel (see also MacGorman, p. 111).

Hagar = slavewoman = Sinai = law = flesh = Jerusalem "now" = mother of slaves
Sarah = freewoman = promise = faith = Spirit = Jerusalem "above" = mother of freemen

In verse 28 Paul clearly states that Christians "are the children of promise." The stronger manuscripts read, "Now you, brethren, as Isaac was, are the children of promise." In the Greek text "you" is emphatic, contrasting them with Jews. The Judaizers were telling these Gentile Christians that for them to be saved they must first become Jews. Paul sets the record straight by emphatically saying that Christians, whether of Gentile or Jewish origin, are the true people of God.

What then is the true state of affairs? Paul answers this by referring to Genesis 21:10 (v. 29). On the occasion of weaning Isaac, Sarah saw Ishmael mocking or mistreating Isaac. So she demanded that Abraham cast out Hagar and her son, "for the son of this bondwoman shall not be heir with my son, even with Isaac." Paul likens this to "persecution" which the children of Ishmael (Jews) continue to carry on against the children of Isaac (Christians). The thought in verse 30 points to the judgment of all Jews and others who remain *sons of Ishmael* by rejecting Christ.

Paul concludes this treatment of law and freedom by declaring, "So then, brethren, we are not children of the bondwoman, but of the free" (v. 31). Note that here he uses *we*. This pronoun can be expanded to include all who truly believe in Christ as their Savior. They are saved by grace through faith (free), not by law plus faith (bondwoman).

The law has its place in God's economy. It is, not the goal, but a roadsign pointing to Christ and to the Father's house. We should not be contented to be chained to the roadsign or to rest in its shadow. Rather we should go beyond it to the freedom which we enjoy as citizens of the "Jerusalem which is above." Even more, we look forward to dwelling in the palace of the King, whose children we are—by his grace and through faith in his Son (Eph. 2:19).

ᚿᚿ 5 ᚿᚿ

Proper Beliefs and Proper Behavior

Galatians 5

TRUE to his normal style, after expounding doctrine Paul applies it. It is important what we believe. But it is equally important that we live according to that belief. *Orthodoxy* must be accompanied by *orthopraxy*. To borrow the title of Foy Valentine's book, we must *believe* and *behave*.

It is possible to commit the Ten Commandments to memory without committing them to life. In such case, one's knowledge of the commandments entails a greater penalty for living in rebellion against them. Now that Paul has so thoroughly proved that Gentiles are saved by grace through faith, it is vitally important that they shall avoid legalism as a means of salvation. Thus he begins chapter 5 with a strong exhortation that they must cling to the gospel of grace.

105

Warning against Legalism (5:1–12)

In 4:21–31 Paul has shown that Christians are the true seed of Abraham through Sarah. As those born of the freewoman, they themselves are free. Therefore, they should not be lured into slavery to law as though they were born of the bondwoman. Now Paul begins this fifth chapter with a ringing call to steadfastness in freedom.

There are various manuscript readings for verse 1. The King James Version places the emphasis upon "stand fast." However, by putting it first in the sentence the Greek text places the emphasis upon the word *freedom,* which Robertson sees as a dative case ("for") rather than an instrumental case ("with"). Thus the reading is "For the freedom Christ set us free." The use of the definite article with "freedom" points to a particular freedom. It is the freedom we enjoy in Christ. Stamm notes that the expression *for freedom* in slightly different Greek form appears in certificates of sacral manumission given to slaves who purchased their freedom. But whereas in those cases each slave paid the price for his freedom, the freedom which Paul has in mind was purchased for us by Christ himself. It is a grace-freedom. He liberated us from Jewish ceremonial law with the purpose that we should remain free. The Judaizers were trying to undo what Christ did.

The secondary emphasis in the sentence is upon *stand fast,* which is linked by *therefore* to the fact which precedes it. Because "for freedom Christ set us free," therefore we are to stand free. Christ provided liberty but we must abide in it. Oscar F. Blackwelder says, "If Christ is the source of grace, freedom is the climax or ripened fruit of grace. Grace and freedom are master words with Paul; all else that he wrote is subhead and detail" (p. 544).

On the negative side of the matter Paul says (literally), "and stop again being held in by a yoke of slavery." The verb rendered *held* ("entangled," KJV) means to be ensnared by a trap. The Judaizers had set a trap for the Galatian Christians, who are urged to keep on avoiding it.

Since circumcision was the basic rite involved in a Gentile's becoming a Jew in religion, Paul begins his argument with it in verse 2 and then relates it to the entire law by which a proselyte must live.

"Behold, I Paul say unto you, that if ye be circumcised, Christ shall profit you nothing" or "nothing at all." Note the emphasis upon *I*—Paul as over against the Judaizers. The "if" clause is a supposable case—it could happen but apparently has not yet done so. Paul is not condemning circumcision as such, for he had been circumcised (Phil. 3:5). He is talking about circumcision as a means of salvation. If you are circumcised as part of following Christ, then you will have forsaken grace for law. And then Christ who saves by grace through faith can do nothing for you. Though he had been circumcised, Paul placed no value upon it as a means to his salvation. In this he is one with Peter, who in Acts 15:11 clearly says that Jews, like Gentiles, must be saved "through the grace of the Lord Jesus." The legalists were saying that Christ helps in our salvation, but that we must through law do our part. Paul says that either Christ alone is the only Savior or else he is no Savior at all.

In verse 3 Paul repeats his witness concerning those who would be saved by legalism. Since he has made no previous statement similar to this in the letter, "again" probably refers to what Paul had told them in person on his first visit to Galatia. He does not say that it is impossible to be saved by keeping the law. In Romans 2:11–16 he has shown that both Jews and Gentiles can be saved thereby. But the catch is that they must keep all the law all the time. The Jew must do this with regard to the written law. The Gentile (pagan) must do the same concerning the law written in his heart. To fail in one law is to be as guilty as if he had failed in all of them (cf. James 2:10–11). And since no man could/would keep the law perfectly, that is precisely the reason why salvation must be by grace through faith.

Paul's mention of circumcision in this verse should not be construed to mean that circumcised Jews could not be saved by grace through faith. Paul himself was such a person. Jewish Christians who had been circumcised before hearing the gospel were exempted from the demands of legalism. The point is that any Gentile who is circumcised as a part of his requirement to be saved becomes a debtor to keep the whole law—without one failure. If one chooses this route there is no halfway point. He must assume the burden of doing the whole law. MacGorman comments, "One cannot be selective in his obedience. The law is not a cafeteria-line where some items may be chosen and others ignored. To admit its validity with respect to circumcision is to place oneself under its total demand" (p. 113). Stamm says, "The sinner's debt *to do the whole law* (KJV) was so crushing that he could only declare himself bankrupt and trust solely to the mercy of the Creator" (p. 547).

The statement of verse 3 is made even more strongly in verse 4. "Christ is become of no effect unto you, whosoever of you are justified by the law; ye are fallen from grace." In the Greek text the verb rendered *is become of no effect* opens the sentence, and so is emphatic. Basically it means to render inoperative. But since the subject is *you* (plural) the verb cannot refer to Christ. It is true that Christ is rendered inoperative for those who seek salvation through legal means. But the sense here is different. The passive voice of the plural verb means that something is being done, not to Christ, but to the Galatians.

In Romans 7:2 and 6, Paul uses the same verb. In verse 2 he states that when a husband dies his wife is discharged from the law which binds her to him. In verse 6, he makes the application that because of Christ's death Christians are discharged from bondage of law. Citing these verses, Robertson gives the verb the meaning of making the law null and void. MacGorman notes that in Romans 7:2 and 6 the movement is from law to grace. Grace annuls the law or makes it null and void. The Revised Standard Version of Galatians 5:4 reads, "You are severed from

Christ"—*from Christ* is a correct rendering of *apo Christou.* So whether we read, "You are discharged from Christ" or "You are severed [separated] from Christ" the sense is the same.

This is true of those who seek to be declared righteous "in the sphere of [*en*] law." *Law* without the definite article involves both the Mosaic code or any other form of legalism. It may even be one's personally devised code of ethics. Such people have "fallen from [out of] grace." *The grace* (there is a definite article in the Greek) refers to a particular kind of grace, God's saving grace in Christ. Being severed from Christ is equivalent to falling out of God's grace.

Some interpreters see this to mean that a person can be in grace and then fall out of grace, or can be saved and then lost again. However, this position is untenable for at least three reasons. (1) It implies that one is saved by works plus faith. Paul's point is that those who rely upon works of *law* are fallen from *grace.* (2) It runs counter to the wide teachings of the New Testament about everlasting life—the permanency of God's life given to us (cf. John 5:24; 10:28–29; Eph. 1:13–14; Col. 3:3). (3) If this means that we can be in grace and then out of grace completely, it contradicts everything else Paul says in this epistle. His overall theme is salvation by grace apart from works of law.

Those holding to the insecurity of the believer also point to such passages as Hebrews 2:1; 3:12; 6:4–6. However, a careful study of the Greek text in these instances shows that the issue is not lost regeneration

but lost opportunity in the Christian life.[1] Even if
Hebrews 6:4–6 teaches a loss of salvation, it also
teaches that once lost it can never be regained. "It is
impossible . . . to renew them again unto repentance."
No repentance, no faith, no salvation. I do not follow
this interpretation. But if you do, then I would
suggest that you get a good hold on your salvation
and never let go. For once lost, it can never again be
regained!

If the author's position be correct, how may we understand Paul's words? Let us suppose that you are
traveling the road toward salvation. You come to a
fork in the road. Pointing toward one road is the sign
Law. Pointing to the other road is a sign *Grace.* You
cannot travel both roads. Which will you choose? If
you choose the Law road, you fall out of or away from
the Grace road. The aorist tense of the verb could be
translated, "You fell out of the grace" or "the grace
road." You cannot be saved by both law and grace.
They cancel out one another. If you choose to be
saved by law or good works, you cannot be saved by
grace, which basically means a gift. By the same token
if you choose the grace way, you cannot follow the law
way. For if you seek to be saved by works, it is by
purchase or merit and not as a gift (Rom. 4:1–5).

Applying all this to the emphatic verb in the verse,
it means that you left the sphere of grace for the
sphere of law. So you are severed from Christ who
saves by grace, not by law. Therefore, in contrast to

1. Herschel H. Hobbs, *How to Follow Jesus* (Nashville: Broadman
Press, 1971), pp. 16–17, 36–39, 58–62.

Romans 7:2, and 6 where Paul describes the severing movement from law to grace, here he says that it is from grace to law. As grace annuls law, so law annuls grace.

Thus Paul carries his warning to its logical and ultimate conclusion. He is not thinking of the occasional sins of a Christian, but of the awful result if you choose to seek justification before God by law, as a substitute for Christ as the means of salvation. It is not a question of being in grace and losing it by a mistake or momentary lapse. It is a matter of choosing whether one will be in grace at all, or will seek salvation by his own ability to keep the moral and ceremonial law of God.

Paul has shown the dismal outcome of depending upon legalism for salvation. Now once again he reminds his readers of their initial experience in Christ (cf. 3:1–5). In the Greek text of verse 5, the first word is an emphatic *we.* It places this verse in sharp contrast with verse 4. Literally, it reads, "We, by the [Holy] Spirit, out of faith [not out of law] a hope of righteousness eagerly await." The hope we are waiting for is characterized by a state of being righteous, that is, justified before God. Being right with God is what gives us hope to the point of assurance as we look toward the final judgment. *Wait* renders a compound verb which *The New English Bible* correctly translates as "we eagerly await."

When we became Christians, the Holy Spirit took up his abode in our lives (John 14:17; 1 Cor. 6:19). In the Book of Acts each time the Holy Spirit is seen coming upon individuals (not the church), his coming is related to the experience of regeneration (8:12, 14–15; 10:44; 19:1–6). In Romans 8:9b Paul says, "Now if any man have not the Spirit of Christ, he is none of his." Thus the indwelling Spirit is a *necessity*, not an *extra* blessing. His indwelling is evidence of regeneration, not of a future sanctification, as some define it.

In the New Testament, the word *salvation* is used to encompass regeneration (Acts 16:30–31), sanctification (Heb. 2:3), and glorification (Heb. 9:28). The split second a person is regenerated he is also sanctified, or set apart as a vessel for God's service. Thus, even though Christians may not always act saintly, they are *saints* (1 Cor. 1:2; 2 Cor. 1:1). The word rendered *saints* in the New Testament may also read "holy ones" or "sanctified ones." We do not grow *into* sanctification; we grow *in the state of* sanctification. Regeneration is the saving of the soul. Sanctification is the saving of the Christian life. Glorification is the sum total of glory and reward in heaven, including the resurrection of the body (Rom. 8:23). In regeneration we are saved from the *penalty* of sin. In sanctification we are being saved from the *power* of sin. In glorification we will be saved from the *presence* of sin. Thus it is correct to say, "I am saved; I am being saved; I will be saved."

This encompassing concept of salvation is what Paul had in mind in Ephesians 1:14, when he spoke of "the redemption [full redemption] of the purchased possession," relating it to the work of the indwelling

Holy Spirit in the preceding verse. The Spirit, here, he calls "the earnest [*arrabōn*] of our [future] inheritance." *Arrabōn* means earnest money or guarantee, and in modern Greek is used for an engagement ring. The word is found only three times in the New Testament (2 Cor. 1:22; 5:5; Eph. 1:14). Each time it is related to the Holy Spirit. All of the above meanings may be seen in Galatians 5:5. We wait through or with the help of the Spirit who is our guarantee and our hope.

Continuing this thought, Paul states that in Christ Jesus neither circumcision nor uncircumcision has strength to enable us to stand justified before God (v. 6). Justification is possible only by the working of faith through God's love for us and our love for him. So both Jews and Gentiles stand on equal footing before God. Whether or not one is circumcised, he must be saved by grace through faith (Acts 15:11). It should be remembered, however, that grace is not "cheap grace," to use Dietrich Bonhoeffer's phrase. It costs God all that he has. And grace makes its demands upon us. Though we are saved by grace through faith, rather than out of ourselves or our good works, as the source, and our salvation is a gift and work of God, we are "created in Christ Jesus *unto good works, which God hath before ordained that we should walk in them*" (Eph. 2:10). Good works are not the *root* but the *fruit* of salvation, and as James says, "Faith without works is dead" (James 2:17).

Now Paul puts a question squarely before his readers (v. 7). "Ye did run well; who did hinder you that ye should not obey the truth?" Literally, "You were running well; who cut in on you?" The former part of the question refers to the time before the Judaizers came on the scene. *Who* is singular. So it apparently refers to some leader among the Judaizers. The Galatian Christians were running well or living beautiful Christian lives. Then this person with his helpers stepped in, either to trip them or lead them out of the right way. The tragedy is that they were in danger of forsaking the truth of the gospel.

Verse 8 is brief, but it is full of meaning. "This persuasion cometh not of him that calleth you." The persuasion or pressure to forsake the gospel of grace certainly did not come from God (1:6). Evidently the Judaizers were saying that they had a higher authority for their message than Paul had for his. The apostle strongly denies this. If the persuasion did not come from God, from whom did it come? Obviously, the answer is the devil. So in perverting the gospel of grace in favor of works plus faith, the Judaizers were serving the devil! He always offers a poor substitute for the real thing. In this light, we can understand better Paul's strong language in 1:6b–9.

Of interest is the fact that *calleth* translates a present participle, "the one keeping on calling." God is still calling them. So Paul urges his readers to turn a deaf ear to the demonic persuaders and to continue running the race of divine truth as set forth in his gospel.

"A little leaven leaveneth the whole lump" (v. 9). This proverb Paul also quotes in 1 Corinthians 5:6. There it has reference to moral impurity. Here it is applied to a perversion of the gospel. With the exception of Matthew 13:33, and its parallel in Luke 13:21, in the New Testament leaven (yeast) is always used as a symbol of evil. The figure here is that of a small portion of yeast spreading throughout a lump of dough. We cannot ignore evil, whether it be moral or spiritual. Broad-mindedness is never a virtue where right and wrong are involved.

While Paul condemns the Judaizers, he also encourages his readers to be true to Christ (v. 10). *I* is emphatic. This emphasis is strengthened by the use of the perfect tense of the verb rendered *have confidence*. It means to persuade. Hence, "I am fully persuaded" or "I have full confidence with respect to you." This expresses a state of mind which he had in the past and continues to have. Even if some had gone over to the Judaizers, apparently most of the Galatian Christians still adhered to the faith.

Paul's basis of confidence was not "through" but "in [*en*] the Lord." He has faith in Christ's holding power which will enable them to stand firm in the gospel. The apostle's appeal is not simply that his readers will be loyal to him, but that they will be in agreement with the gospel he preached to them (cf. vv. 5–6).

On the other hand, "he that troubleth you shall bear his judgment, whosoever he be." The word for *judgment (krima)* expresses the result of the judging process. Of course, this judgment comes from God. The verb is singular. Apparently Paul does not know the identity of the one who is troubling the Galatians, but as the Greek word indicates, they were troubled like an ocean caught in the teeth of a storm. It should be noted, however, that in Galatians 1:7 and 5:12 Paul uses plural forms to refer to the troublemakers. It seems that the problem involved many people, with one singled out as their leader.

In any case, Paul himself is being persecuted by these people, not necessarily physically but by their words (v. 11). Apparently they slandered him by claiming that he also preached circumcision. This could be a distorted interpretation of his act in circumcising Timothy, a half-Jew (Acts 16:3). As noted previously, he did this in order to avoid the possibility of hindering Timothy's work among Jews. It had nothing to do with Timothy's salvation. Paul had already shown in the letter that he refused to have Titus, a Gentile Christian, circumcised (2:3). The fact that the Judaizers opposed Paul so vehemently is proof that their words about him are untrue.

In order to understand Paul's closing words in verse 11, we must note the word rendered *offence*. It is *skandalon*, brought over into English as *scandal*. In 1 Corinthians 1:23 it is translated "stumbling-block." To the Jews, the gospel of a crucified Christ was a *skandalon*. To the Greeks, it was foolishness or moronic (*mōrian*). The Jews looked for a political-military messiah who would destroy their enemies, not be destroyed by them. So they stumbled over the idea of a Savior who died on a cross—a death reserved for the worst of criminals.

The Judaizers were also tainted with this idea. Paul insisted on preaching that Christ crucified was both the power and wisdom of God (1 Cor. 1:24), that faith in him alone was the means of salvation for Jews and Gentiles alike. The Judaizers insisted that Gentiles must become Jews before believing in Christ. So Paul says that if he also preached this message, the cross would no longer be a *skandalon*. *Ceased* renders the same verb translated "is become of no effect" in 5:4. The *skandalon* of the cross would be rendered inoperative, it would become null and void. So the Judaizers' attitude toward him is proof that Paul is still preaching a gospel of grace through faith in a crucified Christ with no element whatever of legalism.

So disturbed is Paul about the Judaizers, that he expresses a wish which is shocking to us (v. 12). Yet when considered in its historical context, it is understandable. "I would they were even cut off which trouble you." Phillips misses the point in an effort to tone down Paul's words: "I wish those who are so eager to cut your bodies would cut themselves off from you altogether." *The Twentieth Century New Testament* reads "mutilate themselves." *The New English Bible* reads "make eunuchs of themselves." Beck's *New Testament in the Language of Today* catches the full meaning: "castrate themselves."

Of course, circumcision involved cutting off a portion of skin of the male sex organ. The Greek *peritomē*, as well as the English *circumcision*, means a cutting around. In Philippians 3:2–3 Paul uses a play on words—"concision" (*katatomēn*, multilation) and "circumcision" (*peritomē*), which approximates his idea here. In effect Paul expresses the wish that those who are so insistent upon circumcising Gentiles would go all the way and emasculate themselves. This is irony, of course, but it has a historical base.

MacGorman points out that in certain pagan religions (e.g., the Cybele-Attis cult) self-emasculation was practiced. "It was the frenzied rite of sacrifice whereby a man entered the priesthood of the cult-goddess" (p. 116). He adds Paul's meaning: "If *circumcusion* is efficacious, then excision ought to be even more so!" Stamm likens this statement within the Christian context to someone who doesn't believe in baptism wishing that those who do would drown themselves (p. 554).

Citing this verse among others, George G. Findlay notes the characteristics of Galatians as "passion and argument . . . hot indignation and righteous scorn . . . tender, wounded affection . . . deep sincerity and manly integrity united with the loftiest consciousness of spiritual authority" (p. 1158). The utterance in 5:12 he calls an "outburst of excessive vehemence" (see also 1:8–9).

However, this strong statement should be seen in its context. Paul is waging a verbal battle in which the prize of war is the souls of men. Furthermore, his God-called ministry is at stake. It is far better that he should express this wish than to keep silent or acquiesce to the Judaizers, and see uncounted multitudes of souls lost in hell eternally. So zealous a man for Christ and men could not fold his spiritual tent and slip away when eternal values were involved.

Warning against Strife (5:13–15)

In these verses Paul faces another problem in the Galatian churches which grew out of the false teaching among them. It was that of strife within their fellowship. Evidently the Christians were taking sides for and against the Judaizers. Opposition from without is one thing; strife within churches is another and more serious matter.

Some interpreters see these words as directed against license or the wrong use of liberty in living as libertines. In Romans 6 Paul deals with the charge that grace is a license to sin. But the context here does not seem to point to what is usually defined as immoral living. "Occasion to the flesh" (v. 13) may better be understood in relation to verse 15.

After the terrible words about the Judaizers, Paul addresses again his readers with the tender word *brethren* (v. 13). He contrasts them to the false teachers, by using an emphatic *you*. In fact *you* is doubly emphatic: it comes first in the Greek sentence, and is written out, as well as being present in the verb form. Christians have been called of God unto or upon (*epi*) freedom. The preposition expresses purpose. The Galatians were not called out of slavery to idols to become slaves to legalism.

However, freedom is accompanied by responsibility. *Liberty* in verse 13b has the definite article. It specifies the freedom which we have in Christ. Therefore, Paul admonishes his readers not to use this freedom as an occasion for the flesh. The verb *use* is not in the Greek text—there is no verb in the sentence, so one must be supplied. Perhaps a better verb is either *convert* or *pervert*. The word translated *occasion* was used in the military sense of a base of operations from which to launch an attack. Only Paul, who was fond of military terms, uses this word in the New Testament (Rom. 7:8, 11; 2 Cor. 5:12; 11:12; 1 Tim. 5:14). The whole phrase is suggestive of strife in the fellowship. But simply because these Christians had been liberated from paganism and legalism was no excuse to abuse their liberty. Freedom of speech calls for controlled emotions and tongues.

The Christian alternative is "by love [to] serve one another." *By* translates *dia,* meaning through—a means of expression. Service is to be "through (the) love" or Christian love *(agapē).* Already Paul had given this advice to the Corinthian church which was torn by strife. This love is the superhighway mentioned in 1 Corinthians 12:31 and explained in 1 Corinthians 13. For any Christian act to have meaning, it must be done in love. W. Hersey Davis once said that the English word which most nearly translates *agapē* is *self-lessness.* When a Christian speaks, he should speak truth, but it should be spoken in the sphere of love (Eph. 4:15). Alas, so many who are involved in theological debate forget this precious gem from the Bible!

It is a paradox that in our Christian experience, we are set free from slavery in order that we may become slaves. The difference is that we are rescued from tyrannical bondage to Satan in order to serve as

Christ's slaves in his benevolent will. One of Paul's favorite terms in self-designation was *a slave of Jesus Christ.*

However, here (v. 13) Paul points out another slavery for Christians: literally, "keep on being slaves to one another." So every Christian is to be a slave to all other Christians. And we are to act through love or through selflessness (Rom. 12:10, 13–21; 1 Cor. 13:4–7). Love "thinketh no evil" (1 Cor. 13:5) means that Christian love does not keep books on the evil done to it with a view to settling the score.

In verse 14 Paul notes that all "the law" is fulfilled in loving one's neighbor as oneself (Lev. 19:18). He makes no reference to loving God absolutely (Deut. 6:5; see Matt. 22:37–40). The first four of the Ten Commandments deal with our relation to God. The last six deal with our relation to other people. Paul is thinking of the Galatian Christians' relation to each other. Hence his reference to loving one's neighbor. Jews defined *neighbor* so as to exclude Samaritans and Gentiles. In the parable of the Good Samaritan, Jesus taught that anyone who needs our help is our neighbor regardless of his background or social status. Certainly Christians should love one another as they love themselves.

Now Paul comes to the crux of the matter. "But if ye bite and devour one another, take heed [beware] that ye be not consumed one of another" (v. 15). The "if" clause assumes that this state of affairs is true. "Bite and devour" describes wild animals fighting among themselves. This is far from the Christian ideal of love. When Christians do this they cause God to weep and Satan to cheer.

The conduct of the Galatians was mutually destructive. They were devouring one another. If this condition continued, the Judaizers would succeed in destroying Paul's work in Galatia. This was added reason for him to be afraid of his readers (4:11). The Judaizers he could handle. But this was quite a different matter. He must have felt like the man who prayed, "Lord, save me from my friends; I can take care of my enemies myself!"

Paul's words remind us of others by Charles Kingsley: "There are two freedoms—the false, where a man is free to do what he likes; the true, where a man is free to do what he ought."

A man had some valuable fox hounds. One day they got into a fight. They were chewing one another to pieces. Seeing his investment destroying itself, he sought to separate them. Time after time he took a dog by his leg and threw him as far as he could. But each dog returned to the fray. Recognizing the futility of his efforts, the man suddenly remembered that he had a fox in a cage. Taking the fox he turned it loose near the dogs. Seeing the fox running away, the dogs lost their difference in their common interest in the fox. They stopped fighting and chased the fox. Every Christian leader should keep a *fox* (program) around to be used on such occasion.

Life in the Spirit (5:16–26)

Instead of walking in the flesh, Paul urges the Galatians to "walk in the Spirit" (v. 16). The Greek word translated *walk* means to walk around and was used figuratively of one's manner of life. Paul used this word thirty-two times in his epistles. We *talk* in the way we *walk*. Living in the Spirit, Paul's readers will not let the desires of the flesh find fulfillment in them. The *not* in this verse translates a strong double negative, and the last phrase could be translated literally, "lust of the flesh you most certainly will not fulfill." The word rendered *lust* means desire—either a good desire (Luke 22:15) or an evil one, as here (cf. James 1:14–15). In James 1:14, "his own lust" probably means a legitimate natural desire; in the next verse it refers to this desire perverted into evil lust.

God has given us natural desires for good purposes. Satan seeks to get us to express them in a way that is contrary to God's will. W. Hersey Davis once defined sin as an illegitimate expression of a legitimate desire. If we walk in the Spirit, we will express these desires according to God's will.

Galatians 5:17 refers to the conflict between desires wrongly expressed and the Holy Spirit. The "flesh lusteth" against the Spirit. Romans 7:14–25 forms a good commentary on this verse. But *desire* in a good sense should be seen in the Spirit's opposition to the flesh. Robertson says, "Christ and Satan long for the possession of the city of Man-Soul as Bunyan shows" (p. 311).

Some interpreters see Paul's words in Romans 7:7–24 as a description of his pre-Christian experience. But the prevalent use of the present tense in the last part of the chapter (vv. 14–25) seems to indicate that he is describing the civil war in his life as a Christian. Verses 7–13 evidently relate his pre-Christian experience. But as is so often the case, the apostle summarizes in Galatians what he treats more fully in Romans. Galatians 5:17 is related to Romans 7:14–25. In verse 18 Paul states what he finally realized in his own Christian life (Rom. 7:24–8:4). "But if ye be led of [by] the Spirit, ye are not under the law." In the Greek text *law* has no definite article, and can mean legalism in any form. The emphasis is upon "if by the Spirit." The "if" clause assumes that the readers are led by the Spirit. Of course, being led by the Holy Spirit, they will live by the law of love.

Paul's words in verses 19–21 do not provide pleasant reading, for in them he lists the works of the flesh, the expressions of unregenerated human nature. They may be listed under three headings: sex (v. 19), worship (v. 20a), and social relationships (vv. 20b–21). Note that each of these are worthy when expressed in God's will. It is when we give in to Satan that they become works of the flesh. *Flesh* here does not refer to matter, but to living according to one's lower, carnal nature.

Sex is a gift of God designed for the good of marriage, home, and family, but when perverted it is a pernicious evil. *Adultery* does not appear in the Greek text. But it is present in the inclusive term *fornication*.

Originally adultery was used of illicit sex which involved one or two married people. Fornication referred to illicit sex between unmarried people. But the latter word came to be used of both premarital and extramarital sex. *Uncleanness* is moral impurity. Out of nine times Paul uses this word, seven are associated with sexual sins. *Lasciviousness* is complete wantonness in sexual behavior.

Worship is also a gift from God. When properly practiced it involves complete communion of our spirits with God. But again Satan seeks to pervert it into all kinds of evil. Under his power men turned to *idolatry* or the worship of idols or gods of their own making. *Witchcraft* renders a Greek word *(pharmakeia)* which referred to drugs or the administering of drugs (the source of our word *pharmacy*). For a period of time, sorcerers came to monopolize the use of drugs in the practice of magical arts associated with idolatry. Pagan religions also practiced sexual perversion in their rites.

Social relationships involve the expression of man's gregarious instinct. Man wants to be with his own kind. Under the Spirit's guidance this results in fellowship, the building of community life, the give and take of sharing goods, services, and the building of a wholesome social order. No man is an island. The highest social values emerge from the fact that as a rule people do not live in isolation.

But when Satan is given power in human relations, he turns a paradise into a jungle. It may be a jungle of concrete, steel, and stone. But it is a jungle just the same. Paul describes such a tragedy in verses 20b–21. *Hatred* means enmity. *Variance (eris)* means strife, discord. In Greek religion Eris was the goddess of strife. She was the sister of Ares, the god of war. *Emulations* means burning zeal. In the bad sense as here it means jealousy. *Wrath* means boiling rage. It was used of the rapid burning of dry grass. It flares up but soon subsides, like the eruption of a volcano. *Strife* means factions or organized self-interest. *Seditions* connotes divisions. *Heresies* refers to party strife. *Envyings* may read either jealousies or feelings of ill-will. *Murders* does not occur in the best texts. *Drunkenness* is excessive drinking. It is accompanied by *revellings* or carousing. *The New English Bible* renders these last two words as "drinking bouts [held in honor of the wine god Bacchus], orgies."

The works of the flesh are quite a kettle of rotten fish! For a fuller treatment of these read Romans 1:22–32. Since Paul wrote both of these letters from Corinth, he may well be describing the pagan life of that wicked city. The name of that city became synonymous with wickedness—"to corinthianize" (like "sodomy") described a person's sinking to the lowest depths of moral evil.

Paul adds a reminder of what he had previously told his readers in person. Literally, "the ones practicing such things will not inherit the kingdom of God." "The ones practicing" renders a present participle—those who make such things the habit of their lives. Of course, a person may be saved from such things through faith in Jesus Christ.

Against this dark background of evil, Paul lists "the fruit of the Spirit" (vv. 22–23), which appears more glorious by contrast. Note the singular *fruit*. The following Christian virtues are like a cluster of grapes. These ethical principles are produced inwardly by the indwelling Holy Spirit, and they find outward expression in the lives of Spirit-controlled believers. Legalism cannot produce such fruit, any more than hanging apples on a thorn bush can change it into an apple tree. The process of production is from inward to outward, not from outward to inward.

MacGorman says, "No law has been given which is able to make alive (3:21b); it can only instruct, require, and provoke. What is needed is a dynamic commensurate with the demand. For the Christian this dynamic derives from the Spirit who produces fruit in him (cf. Matt. 7:16–20; Luke 6:43–45; John 15:1–8)" (p. 119).

Paul lists nine parts of this fruit. *Love*, as we have noted, is selflessness. It characterizes the very nature of God (1 John 4:8). It is that which comes from God to us, and in faith in his Son from us to God, and which in Christ we should extend to all men (1 John 4:9–11). It is downward, upward, and outward—and by following these directions we make the sign of the cross. The greatest expression of God's love is seen at Calvary (Rom. 5:8). Love is self-giving. It does not ask, "What must I give?" but "What may I give?" This virtue is generated and developed in us by the power of the indwelling Spirit.

Joy renders a word *(chara)* which is akin to grace

(charis). Joy inevitably accompanies love. It is more than happiness which is determined by happenings or outward circumstance. Rather it is serenity in the midst of a storm (Matt. 5:11–12). The keynote of Paul's epistle to the Philippians is joy (1:4, 25; 2:2, 29; 4:1, 4, 11–12)—and he wrote it while a prisoner in Rome.

Peace is related to joy. It is an inner calm which rises above outward environment and experience. In all of Paul's salutations he uses *grace* and *peace.* The order is correct. Once we experience God's grace, we know his peace. It is not the peace which the world may give and take away, but the abiding gift of Christ (John 14:27). Despite tribulation, Christians know this peace because Christ has fully conquered the world, and we know victory in him (John 16:33).

Longsuffering means that one suffers long the evil done to him without retaliation, and is "long-tempered" rather than short-tempered. One keeps a long fuse on his temper. The natural man is prone toward outbursts of rage (5:20b). But the Spirit teaches patience in the Christian's life.

Gentleness or kindness goes a step beyond longsuffering. It is a positive and active quality rather than a negative and/or passive one. It seeks to do good to one who has wronged it (Matt. 5:44; 1 Cor. 13:4; 2 Cor. 6:1–6).

Goodness is "benevolence" (Weymouth) or "generosity" (Phillips). It involves more than moral freedom from evil, but is positive and aggressive, as the Christian seeks to be good-for-something. It is being a light in darkness, food for the hungry, water for the thirsty, as one lets the light of Christ shine through him. It is serving God by serving men (Matt. 25:35–40).

Faith is fidelity, dependability. As God is faithful to us (1 Cor. 1:9) so should we be faithful to him (1 Cor. 15:58). Our word should be our bond (Matt. 5:37). Christians should be devoted to duty, and should have the distinction of reliability among their fellowmen.

Meekness today connotes weakness. But the Greek word which it translates is a strong word. "Gentle strength" (MacGorman) more adequately expresses its meaning (cf. Matt. 11:29). MacGorman quotes William Barclay (*Flesh and Spirit,* pp. 120–21): "Only a *praus* [meek person] could have both cleansed the Temple of the hucksters who traded in it and forgiven the woman taken in adultery whom all the orthodox condemned."

A *meek* person is a teachable person, not a know-it-all. The word is used of breaking a horse in order to use it. The purpose is not to break its spirit but to harness its power. So meekness is power under control.

Temperance means self-control. In the New Testament it is used only here and in Acts 24:25 and 2 Peter 1:6. It connotes inner strength by which one controls himself, using his powers for good and not bad. A temperate person does not drift with the current of evil social practices; he dares to stand up against them as he stands out for God and right. It is significant that Paul begins with love or selflessness and closes with self-control. They are like parentheses enclosing and making possible the other virtues.

Of further significance is the fact that the fruit of the Spirit deals with inner graces. Conspicuous by their absence are the ecstatic gifts of the Spirit upon which some people place such great value.

Paul closes this list by noting that "against such there is no law." As legalism cannot produce these virtues, neither are laws necessary to protect others from those who possess them. For "they that are Christ's [of Christ Jesus] have crucified [aorist tense, a definite historical event] the flesh [forces which make for evil] with the affections [passions] and lusts" or perverted desires (v. 24).

The apostle concludes this chapter with two exhortations. "If we live in the Spirit, let us also walk in the Spirit. Let us not be desirous of vain glory, provoking one another, envying one another" (v. 25–26). The "if" clause assumes that his readers are living in the Spirit, referring to inner spiritual life. Since this is true, they should "walk in the Spirit." Many translations use *by* rather than *in* in both cases. However, since Paul is thinking of an inner mystical union, *in* seems to be the better reading. *The New English Bible* reads, "If the Spirit is the source of our life, let the Spirit also direct our course."

The word rendered *walk* is not the usual one used by Paul (*peripateō*, 5:16). It is *stoicheō*. It means to walk in line or in step. We should walk a straight path in fellowship with the Holy Spirit. If we do this we will not seek the empty glory of the world. Neither will we provoke or envy one another. The verb rendered *provoking* means to call forth. In the bad sense, as here, it means to challenge someone to combat. So this takes us back to the warning issued in 5:13–15.

Spirit-controlled Christians will enjoy spiritual fellowship. They will be so busy working for the Lord and his glory that they will not be tempted to battle among themselves. Kicking mules never pull, and pulling mules never kick. When hounds are chasing a *fox* they are not devouring one another. Christians can learn much from such animals.

6

Exhortation and Summary

Galatians 6

THE FIRST ten verses of Galatians 6 are actually a continuation of chapter 5. The next seven verses constitute Paul's autograph as he summarizes the message of the entire epistle. In chapter 5 he has nailed down his argument for freedom as opposed to legalism (vv. 1–12), has appealed for harmony in church fellowship (vv. 13–15), and has urged his readers to avoid the works of the flesh and to walk in the Spirit who would bear his fruit in them (vv. 16–26). As we seek to understand 6:1–10, we must keep in mind particularly the apostle's words in 5:13 to 26.

Mutual Helpfulness (6:1–10)

One of the great hymns of Christian fellowship—"Blest Be the Tie that Binds"—catches the sense of what Paul is saying in these verses.

We share our mutual woes,
    Our mutual burdens bear;
And often for each other flows
    The sympathizing tear.

—JOHN FAWCETT

Other than the family circle, there is no closer fellowship than that of church relationships. But as in a family, along with the blessedness there is the possibility of strife. That this was an actual danger, if not a reality in these Galatian churches, is seen in 5:13–15. Furthermore, to change the figure, every flock has its strong sheep as well as its weak, if not black ones. So viewing the churches as flocks of God, Paul is concerned that in Galatia the strong should help the weak. His urgency in this matter is evident in that in these ten verses he uses ten imperative verbs.

Though the churches in Galatia were a present heartache to Paul, he repeatedly addresses them as *brethren* (1:2, 11; 3:15; 4:12, 28, 31; 5:11, 13; 6:1, 18). His tone at times may be harsh, but he wants them to know that he speaks in love. They are his brethren in the Lord. Paul's only singular form of this word (*adelphon*, 1:19) refers to James as the Lord's "brother" or half-brother. *Adelphos* comes from another Greek word, meaning out of the same womb. Since Christians have the same source of spiritual life they are "brethren." All men are created by God. He is fatherly in his nature, and longs to be the Father of all men. But he is Father in truth only of those who have become his sons through faith in his Son Jesus Christ

(John 1:12). In this light, therefore, Christians not only are parts of the church fellowship; they also are members of the family of God.

Now as such they should have mutual concern for each other. So Paul says that if one of them is overtaken in a fault, those who are Spirit-controlled should restore him (v. 1a). *Overtaken* translates a verb that means to take beforehand. Its derived meaning is to surprise or detect. The sense here is that of detecting one in a *fault*. The Greek word means a falling aside. The idea is that of "trespass" (RSV). Williams translates it, "the very act of doing wrong." This falling aside should be interpreted in the light of Paul's use of the word *walk* in 5:25. The fault may be moral (cf. 5:17–21) or reference may be to a person snared by the Judaizers (4:17; 5:26).

Paul asks the spiritual in the group to help the person detected in a fault. The *spiritual* "refers not to any special order of 'spiritual men' *('pneumatics')*, but potentially to any believer who is fulfilling 5:25" (F. Roy Coad, p. 455). They should restore him. The verb translated *restore* was used of a physician setting a broken bone. It is used in Matthew 4:21 for mending nets. But the former sense seems to be preferable here. Here is the first of a series of imperatives Paul issues in these verses. Whatever the "fault" may be, the spiritual brethren should restore the offender's conduct as gently and effectively as a physician would set a broken leg. He does not beat the broken leg or the patient. He treats it so that the person may be strong again.

This should be done "in the spirit of meekness; considering thyself, lest thou also be tempted." *Thou* is emphatic setting the one addressed over against the offender. Rather than condemning the wayward brother, each one should learn from his experience. Note here that Paul moves from the plural *brethren* to the singular *thyself.* Frederic Rendall sees this transition to mean that "the treatment of offenders belonged to the Church collectively, but each member needed to examine himself individually, in order that he might fulfil his part with due humility and sympathy" (p. 189). This is true. But there is more. Each Christian should deal gently with offenders, knowing that he could find himself in their place. One should not indulge in Pharisaical pride (Luke 18:11). He should ask how he would stand the same tempting or testing. The situation could be reversed. In essence Paul is saying that in dealing with others we should apply the Golden Rule.

This dual truth the apostle applies in verses 2–5. In the Greek text *one another's burdens* opens the sentence and so is emphatic. *Bear* is a present imperative, and can be translated "keep on bearing." This verb is used of Jesus bearing his cross (John 19:17). In reality the cross was ours, but he bore it as his own. It is in this spirit that we should bear the burdens of others. The word for *burdens (barē)* connotes a crushing load which one is unable to bear alone. This exhortation does not exempt the one with the burden from burden-bearing (2 Cor. 8:13), but means rather that stronger Christians should lend a hand in helping him from being destroyed by it.

The *burdens* here are a particular burden of a fault (v. 1) either a lapse in morals or faith. But the thought may be enlarged to include any crushing burden: e.g., economic need, responsibility, or grief. In these and other instances, Christians have been strengthened in their faith in and dedication to God when helped through life's crises by fellow-believers.

When we help another Christian with his burden, we are fulfilling the law of Christ. This law is the law of love as seen in 5:13b–14. The Greek verb rendered *fulfil* is a compound word meaning to fill up. It complements the perfect tense of the basic verb in 5:14— again the idea is to fulfill completely that law. This is not legalism but Christian love in action. It is living according to the Ten Commandments and the Golden Rule, not as an aid to salvation but as an expression of it. *One another's* applies especially to the Christian fellowship, but it extends beyond that to include all people (cf. v. 10).

As verse 2 corresponds to verse 1a, so verses 3–4 correspond to verse 2b. If the one who is not guilty of a fault takes the prideful attitude that he is someone—that is, that he is better than the guilty person—when actually he is nothing, he deceives himself (v. 3). The verb translated *deceiveth* is formed from the word for *mind* and the verb *to lead astray.* In other words, such a person is leading his mind astray. Such a person is guilty of empty glory (5:26). He sets up his own standard of goodness, the norm being himself. He is like one who looks into a mirror in order to find the perfect man (2 Cor. 10:12; James 1:23–24). If some people could buy themselves in the morning for what they are worth, and in the afternoon sell themselves for what they think they are worth, they would make a fortune in a day. Such a person, says Paul, lives in a delusion. He is really a *zero*—this is the sense of *nothing*. (While 1 Cor. 13:2 uses a different word for *nothing*, the sense is the same.)

Rather than comparing himself with others, a person should take inventory of himself (v. 4). Human nature leads us to condemn sins in others that we condone in ourselves. We should be as honest in self-appraisal as we are when we judge others. "Let every man prove his own work." *Prove* means to prove genuine or false by testing, as with metals. We should not use one standard for others and a different one for ourselves. In this verse, the Greek begins with, and therefore emphasizes, the phrase "but his own work," and a present imperative verb follows. The present tense means that this proving should be a continuing process. Rather than expressing censorious criticism of others, we should keep our motives and works under the microscope of self-analysis. A sign in a beauty salon reminded ladies to watch their figures, for others were doing it. The Christian should keep his eyes on his own life, for the world is keeping its eyes on him. And strangely, the world

expects more of Christian people than most of them
expect of themselves.

The prepositions in verb 4b are *eis*. They may be
translated into or with respect to. Two thoughts
emerge about this. One is that one should be able to
rejoice, glory, or "boast" (RSV) with respect to his own
successes rather than with respect to the failures of
another. Moffatt translates this, "Then he will have
something to boast about on his own account, and not
in comparison with his fellows." Equally significant is
the idea that if one has something of which to boast, it
should be done within himself and not to others.
There is a saying that it is fine for a person to be
smart, provided he doesn't find it out. But even if he
does recognize it, this should be grounds for thanking
God for his grace rather than telling others about
smartness. If you are good or smart, others will find it
out. If you are not, then all of your telling it will not
make it so.

Verse 5 creates a problem in English. It seems to
contradict verse 2. However, in the Greek text two
different words for *burden* are given (see discussion of
verse 2). In verse 5 *burden* renders a word *(phortion)*
used variously of a ship's cargo (Acts 27:10), the burden of the law (Matt. 23:4), and a soldier's pack. Jesus
used this word when he spoke of his burden as being
light (Matt. 11:30). By comparison, the Pharisees'
burden of legalism is heavy because they place it upon
others but lend no aid in bearing it (Matt. 23:4). The
words *barē* (v. 2) and *phortion* (v. 5) were sometimes

used interchangeably. But here Paul makes a distinction between crushing burdens and those burdens that a person can bear alone. Those we can bear alone we should not impose upon others.

Whether his burden be a moral one of guilt, or one of responsibility, each person is responsible for bearing his own burden. Phillips catches the sense here: "For every one must 'shoulder his own pack.'" If a person needs help, Christians should give it in Christian love. But no one should seek to shift his pack onto another's shoulders.

"Let him that is taught in the word communicate unto him that teacheth in all good things" (v. 6). Here Paul points out a specific burden that Christians should help another bear. As the work of the churches grew, teachers were necessary to give religious instruction to those who believed in Jesus. Their teaching duties left them no time to earn a livelihood. So this had to be provided by others. Who but those being taught should provide this? Thus the burden of teaching was borne by both the teachers and the ones taught.

While recognizing that those who preach the gospel should live by it, be provided for by other Christians (2 Cor. 9:14), Paul supported himself in order to refute the criticism of the Judaizers that he preached for money (Acts 18:1–3; 1 Cor. 9:6–18; 2 Cor. 11:7–11; 1 Thess. 2:6, 9). Only the Philippian church is reported as helping him financially (Phil. 4:14–18).

Paul did not ask for their financial help, but when it came he gladly received it because he knew that they gave it out of love. The Philippians were partners with Paul in the gospel, just as every Christian may be with those who serve the Lord without time to earn a living otherwise, when he gives to support them.

Communicate renders an imperative verb meaning to share, which is also the root of the word translated *fellowship*. It is emphatic in the Greek text. *Contribute* would be a better translation here. As the teachers shared their spiritual wisdom, so those being taught should share their financial resources. This is mutual burden-bearing.

However, two words of caution are appropriate here. For one thing, it is utterly ridiculous to charge that a person in a religious vocation does it for the money. After almost a half-century in the ministry, I can say that if any minister should invest in any other work the same amount of talent, time, and energy that he puts into the ministry, he could double, triple, or more his income. In the second place, no Christian should feel that he is *paying* someone else to do *his* work for the Lord. To the obligation of mutual burden-bearing is the added burden of one's own responsibility to the Lord which only he/she can bear.

The phrase *In all good things* broadens the idea of *burden* beyond material things. It involves prayer, support, and being a fellow-laborer with others in the gospel. MacGorman is right when he says, "The very indefiniteness of the phrase leaves open the broad range of commonality which may find catechist [teacher] and catecumen [the one taught] together" (p. 121).

At first glance, verses 7–8 seem to be reinforcement for verse 6. It is true that one receives back in degree and kind that which he sows or gives (2 Cor. 9:6). But it hardly seems possible to limit the meaning of the verses to the idea of giving. The use of *flesh* and *Spirit* ties these evident truths to Paul's words about this contrast in 5:16–6:6. He has warned against works of the flesh and urged that his readers walk in the Spirit. This latter he applies to relationships within the church fellowship. As he rushes to conclude the body of the letter, Paul lays down this axiom from natural law to illustrate the spiritual principle involved (cf. Job 4:8). The principle is true whether it involves moral or spiritual conduct, whether it be viewed corporately or personally.

"Be not deceived; God is not mocked: for whatsoever a man soweth, that shall he also reap" (v. 7).

The verb rendered *deceived (planaō)* is the one from which the word *planet* is derived. The ancients thought of the planets as errant, wandering bodies. Hence the idea of being deceived or led astray. The present passive imperative verb preceded by the negative particle *mē* means "stop being led astray." The readers were already being led astray and should stop following the wrong path and the wrong leader. The verb translated *mocked* means to turn up the nose in scorn. The point is that you cannot turn up your nose at God and get away with it. This does not mean that people do not mock God. It means that they do not do it with impunity. They pay a terrible price for doing so.

This Paul expresses in the inexorable law of nature. "Whatsoever a man soweth, that shall he also reap." Many years ago on "The Baptist Hour," I preached a sermon on verses 7 and 8 using the topic "Every Farmer Knows This." Yes, every farmer knows that if he sows corn he will harvest corn. He does not sow weeds and expect to reap wheat. He knows and respects nature's law. Yet that same person often will sow evil deeds without expecting to reap the same.

The same God who made natural law also made physical, moral, and spiritual law. For our good he operates his universe by law, not by whim and caprice, else the farmer would not know when or what to plant in order to achieve a desired result. But because he knows what harvest he desires, he also knows when and what seed to plant. He looks ahead to the end before making a beginning—knowing that God's natural laws are reliable.

If only we would be as wise in the other seed we sow! You cannot sow indulgence and reap health. You cannot sow strife and reap peace. You cannot sow sin and reap righteousness. You cannot sow "the works of the flesh" and reap "the fruit of the Spirit."

A further truth is that we not only reap what we sow in *quality*, but that we reap more than we sow in *quantity*. If you plant one grain of corn you will harvest corn. But from the one seed you will reap hundreds of like grains. Is it any wonder that so many lives are blasted, that the world is in constant turmoil, or that souls by the uncounted millions stumble on their blinded way toward hell!

In verse 8 Paul moves from the realm of nature into that of the Spirit. If we sow to the flesh we shall "of the flesh reap corruption" or rottenness. Robertson says, "Nature writes in one's body the penalty of sin as every doctor knows" (p. 316). Yes, and history writes the same story about social orders and nations. And the pages of eternity tell the far more terrible story about the souls of men. If only we would set our desired goals at the beginning, and not be led astray by the devil!

On the other hand, if we sow to the things of the Spirit, we "shall of [out of] the Spirit reap life everlasting." *Life everlasting* may be translated "spiritual life of the age" or age-abiding life. The adjective means *perpetual,* as seen in the writings of Plato. The Greek language has no stronger word *(aiōnios)* to express eternity (John 3:16). The only way to strengthen it is to repeat it: "unto the ages of the ages" *(eis tous aiōnas tōn aiōnōn,* Gal. 1:5; Rev. 22:5). Eternal life is measured in terms of quality, not quantity. It is not a life which the Christian receives the moment he dies physically. It is the quality of life which he has now and which abides in eternity. But we can enhance the quality here and now and in eternity by permitting the Holy Spirit to bear his fruit in our lives.

I used to wonder why the final judgment comes at the end of the age. Why not render final judgment for each person the first second after death? It finally occurred to me that a judge cannot render final and righteous judgment until all the evidence is in. All the *evidence* or fruit of our lives will not be in until the

Lord comes again. The final judgment will not determine who are saved and who are lost. That condition is fixed at the moment of death or, if one is still alive, when Jesus returns. The judgment will only declare that state (Rev. 20:12–15). Those whose names are written in "the book of life" will be in heaven. All others will be in hell. But "they were judged every man according to their works" (Rev. 20:13b). This will be a judgment based on our *works,* not on God's grace through faith or lack of it in his Son. This judgment will determine *degrees* of reward in heaven (Matt. 25:14–46) and of punishment in hell (Luke 12:47).

A person commits what society calls a little sin. But that little sin sets in motion evil forces which by the end of the age will result in millions of souls going to hell. Another person gives a cup of cold water in the Savior's name. A little thing to be sure. But that simple act will set in motion good forces which by the end of the age will result in millions of souls trusting in Jesus. Little seeds, but what great harvests! Yes, we reap what we sow in quality—but infinitely more in quantity.

Every farmer knows the necessity for the patience of waiting between seedtime and harvest. He also knows the toil of cultivation. Christians need to learn the same lesson. The results of sowing to the Spirit are not always readily apparent. But "in due season we shall reap, if we faint not" (v. 9). The verb translated *faint* means to loosen out, to become relaxed, lackadaisical, or exhausted. We must not let Satan do this to us. *Due season* means "its own opportune time."

This time is the harvest time, whenever that may be.

Many years ago on a Sunday night, a young man was saved. A lady with tearful eyes said to me, "I taught him as a boy in Sunday school. Try as I did, I could not lead him to Christ. But I have never ceased to pray for him to be saved. At times I felt that God must be weary from my prayers. Now I know that he was not." The opportune time came because she did not faint or quit praying.

Paul closes his dictation with a word of exhortation (v. 10). *Opportunity* translates the same word rendered *season* in verse 9. "So then, as we have opportunity, let us keep on working the good to all, but especially to the ones of the household of faith" (literal). We do good to all men as a witness for Christ, and to the household of faith for a growing, enriched fellowship of mutual helpfulness.

Summation of the Epistle (6:11–16)

In all likelihood the first letters Paul wrote were 1 and 2 Thessalonians. Apparently between these two someone had sent a forged letter in his name (2 Thess. 2:2). To avoid such an occurrence in the future, Paul took the pen after dictating 2 Thessalonians and wrote a few words himself to show that the letter was authentic. "The salutation of Paul with mine own hand, which is the token in every epistle: so I write" (2 Thess. 3:17). Or "It is the way I write" (RSV). Note 1 Corinthians 16:21; Galatians 6:11; Colossians 4:18; Philemon 19. "Morris (p. 151) notes that the fact that Paul says nothing about it in other letters does not mean that he did not always do it, but that he did not emphasize it."[1] In this light we may understand Galatians 6:11–16. Not only did he authenticate the letter, but in his own hand he added a summary of the entire epistle. He wanted to assure his readers that the message of this letter was authentic, regardless of what the Judaizers might say to the contrary.

"Ye see how large a letter I have written unto you with mine own hand" (v. 11).

Paul does not mean that he wrote the entire epistle by hand. The length of Galatians does not fit the idea of a large or long letter. The verb rendered *have written* is an epistolary aorist form. This denotes the *act* of the writer at the time, not what he has written. It should read, "I am writing" (RSV). Also *letter* is dative plural, so it means "letters." Stamm rightly calls it an instrumental dative, "You see with what large letters I am writing to you with my hand."

This seems to refer to the distinctive way Paul formed his letters. Some see the reference to large letters as evidence that Paul had poor eyesight. Others note his crude or printed letters in contrast to the expert penmanship of the scribe or amanuensis. The former of these is pure conjecture. The latter seems unlikely in the light of Paul's scholarship and familiarity with the Greek language. Moulton and

---

1. Herschel H. Hobbs, *Commentary on 2 Thessalonians,* The Broadman Bible Commentary, vol. 11 (Nashville: Broadman Press, 1971), p. 298; see Leon Morris, *The Epistles of Paul to the Thessalonians,* Tyndale Bible Commentary (Grand Rapids: Wm. B. Eerdmans, 1968).

Milligan, while admitting the possibility that the latter may be the case, also note the practice of using large letters to call attention to an announcement on a board. They state that "this may illustrate emphasis as the cause" of the large letters in verse 11.[2]

It seems likely, therefore, that Paul deliberately used large printed letters, like bold-faced type, in order to call attention to what he is about to write. MacGorman says, "Thus the boldness of the handwriting at the end matches the boldness of the letter throughout" (p. 123). He wanted his readers—and the Judaizers—to *get the message*.

For at least two reasons, writes Paul in his own handwriting, the Galatian Christians should not trust the Judaizers. For one thing, they wanted Gentiles to be circumcised and become Jewish proselytes before believing in Jesus, so that they themselves might escape persecution from other Jews (v. 12). Paul was persecuted because he taught that faith in Christ crucified was all that was necessary for Gentiles to be saved (5:11). Judaism could have accepted Christianity simply as a branch of their faith. Indeed, until the fall of the Jewish nation in A.D. 70 it was so regarded by the Romans. But to make it an altogether separate faith which centered in a crucified and risen Jesus Christ, was too much. No matter that the Judaizers regarded Jesus as the Messiah, if they could report the large number of Gentiles they had led to be circumcised and become a part of Judaism, it would

---

2. James H. Moulton and George Milligan, *The Vocabulary of the Greek New Testament* (Grand Rapids: Eerdmans, 1949), p. 131.

soften the blow to the Jews about Christ. Thus Paul accuses them of selfish motives. They were trying to ride two horses going in opposite directions.

In the second place, the apostle accuses the Judaizers themselves, though circumcised, of not living by the Mosaic code (v. 13). Yet they insist that the Galatians do both. Their only motive is that they may glory in their flesh. They have no real concern for their spiritual salvation. The word rendered *flesh* is not the usual one *(sarx)*. Here it means "that which is yours." This refers to their circumcision. Williams reads "so that they can boast of you as members of their party." *The Living Bible* says, "In order that they can boast that you are their disciples." The Judaizers were not interested in what they could do for these Gentiles after circumcision. Or as someone said of some Sunday schools, "They only count noses and nickels"—what is the attendance and offering? They are like some preachers who want baptisms for baptisms' sake, regardless of whether a person is saved or not. The Judaizers had their eyes on statistics rather than on souls.

In contrast to the Judaizers, Paul says, "But God forbid that I should glory, save in the cross of our Lord Jesus Christ, by whom the world is crucified unto me, and I unto the world" (v. 14). He not only declares this in exultation, but also in revulsion over the fleshly motives of his enemies. In the Greek, this verse begins with the words *to me,* which emphasizes the contrast in motives.

Note Paul's familiar "God forbid." Let no idea or

motive come into being, but that he gloried in the cross and in Christ crucified as the only means of salvation. "By whom" (KJV) makes the words that follow refer to Christ. The Revised Standard Version reads "by which," referring to the cross. In the Greek text the relative pronoun may read either way. And in the final analysis both are true. But the context (vv. 12b, 14b) seems to favor "by which." Paul did not say, "Christ crucified" but "the cross of . . . Christ." Frederic Rendall says; "He will glory only in the triumph of the cross over his own flesh [not the Galatians' through circumcision], whereby the power of the world over him, and his carnal love of the world, are both done away" (p. 191). In retrospect when Christ died, Paul died. Yet as Christ lives on, so does he live on (2:19–20).

MacGorman puts it in striking words. "It is not that the Judaizers gloried and Paul did not. Rather it is that the Judaizers gloried in the flesh of the Galatians, whereas Paul gloried in the cross of the Galilean" (p. 124).

The best manuscripts of verse 15 do not have "in Christ Jesus," even though the idea itself is involved. The cross avails only for those who are "in Christ" through faith in him. But the best Greek text reads, "For neither circumcision is anything nor uncircumcision, but a new creation." In other words, the cross removes the distinction between Jews and Gentiles. A Jew is not saved because he is circumcised; a Gentile is not lost because he is not circumcised. If the cross be rightly understood, it makes both conditions without meaning. What God demands for salvation is neither of these. He demands a new creation, a new person, not once-born but twice-born. In 2 Corinthians 5:17 Paul said, "Therefore if any man be in Christ, he is a new creature [creation]: old things are passed away; behold, all things are become new."

Paul expresses the wish for peace and mercy upon all who walk (in a straight line, 5:25) according to the rule laid down in verse 15 (v. 16). "And upon the Israel of God." Here *and (kai)* should read "even." So Paul identifies Christians as the true Israel of God— not those who are circumcised and live by legalism, but those who are new creations by grace through faith in Jesus Christ. This final phrase really zeroes in on the Judaizers and on all who would add anything to grace through faith in Christ as a means of salvation. God's true Israel is not made up of circumcised legalists but of free men and women in Christ (cf. 1 Pet. 1:1–10).

We can see why Paul wrote these words himself. There must be no mistake, no doubt as to what constitutes the true gospel.

Parting Words (6:17–18)

The rather abrupt ending of Galatians is most suggestive. It had not been easy to write this letter. So he must have been spent emotionally. But in two verses he has a parting word, first, for his opponents, and, then, for his friends.

"From henceforth let no man trouble me: for I bear in my body the marks of the Lord Jesus" (v. 17). The best Greek texts do not have "Lord."

Paul has fully answered the Judaizers. So he says to them that from now on (literally, "for what remains") he does not want to hear any more from them. The verb portion of the phrase translated *trouble* basically means to have alongside. It was used in the sense of furnish or cause. Together with a noun meaning difficulty or hardship it forms a phrase meaning bother someone, annoy, cause trouble.[3]

Marks renders the word *stigmata,* plural of *stigma,* which has been brought over into English as a mark of shame or dishonor. It may be rendered "brand marks," with the same idea as the modern practice of branding cattle. In ancient times it was sometimes the custom to brand slaves or, at times, even soldiers. A soldier might brand himself with his commander's insignia to show his loyalty. Arndt and Gingrich note the practice of religious tattooing (p. 776).

However, Paul regarded his *stigmata* of Jesus as marks not of dishonor but of honor. He referred to his scars resulting from stonings, beatings, and probably from manacles and leg irons (cf. Acts 14:19; 16:23–24; 2 Cor. 1:8–10; 6:4–10; 11:23–33). They were the marks of his slavery to Christ, faithful service in the face of extreme difficulty, and scars of a good soldier of Jesus Christ. These *stigmata* spoke more eloquently of Paul's faithfulness as an apostle

---

3. See W. F. Arndt and F. W. Gingrich, "kopos," and "parecho" (Chicago: University Press, 1957), pp. 444, 632.

than any words he could utter. Let the Judaizers display theirs if they had any! Even if the Galatians wavered between their words and Paul's, they surely should believe his scars.

A missionary in Burma had been tortured and put in prison. The torture left his hands a mass of scars. At long last he asked for permission to present his case before the country's ruler. His request was denied, but he was told that someone else might plead his case. When he asked what was the difference, he was told that the ruler would probably not believe someone's words on his behalf, but he could not fail to believe the scars. (Obviously, he did not want to believe.)

In this age of easy Christianity, it is difficult for us to identify with Paul. Some may bear inward scars resulting from scorn, intimidation, and even being ignored in their witness for Christ. But Paul's scars stood out for all to see, and bore personal witness to his loyalty to Christ.

A story is told out of the life of Julius Caesar. When he defeated Pompey in battle, Pompey fled to Egypt for safety, and Caesar followed him there. Thinking to please Caesar, the Egyptian ruler beheaded Pompey and had his head presented on a platter to the Roman. When Caesar saw it, he viewed not his fallen foe but his vanquished kinsman. So he declared war on Egypt.

Not anticipating trouble, he had led only a small contingent of troops to Egypt. As a result he might have lost the war, except for the help of Antipater, the father of Herod the Great, who organized an army of Jews from Alexandria, and helped Caesar win the war.

After the war, Antigonus, the rival of Antipater for power in Judea, appeared before Caesar and warned him not to trust Antipater, who, he said, was personally ambitious and loyal to no one but himself. Hearing these charges, Julius Caesar asked Antipater for his reply to the charges. Slowly Antipater loosened his waistcoat and drew it back, revealing a mass of scars on his body. Then he said, "These scars were gained fighting the battles of Caesar." He said no more. Nor did he need to. The scars spoke more clearly than words.

This is something of the meaning of Paul's statement. It was his crowning reply to his adversaries.

Then Paul wrote a brief parting word to his friends. "Brethren, the grace of our Lord Jesus Christ be with your spirit. Amen" (v. 18). Not the legalism of Moses but "the grace of our Lord Jesus Christ."

The uniqueness of this benediction among all of Paul's letters is that here he concludes it with the word *brethren*. The King James Version opens the verse with this word. But the Greek text closes with it, followed only by "Amen." The problem-Christians in the churches of Galatia were still Paul's *brethren*. He deliberately placed this word here to emphasize this fact. Long after they had heard this letter read in their churches, the word *brethren* would be ringing in their ears. It forms an abiding link of spiritual oneness between this perplexed apostle and his troubled children in the Lord.

Christian people may at times differ on vital spiritual issues. In moments of emotion they may even speak harshly. But speaking truth as they see it, they should do so in love. They should never forget that they are brethren in the Lord.

The first Baptist World Congress met in London in 1905. Dr. A. H. Strong, one of the profoundest theologians of the United States, delivered the Congress sermon. While stressing the unity of Baptists, he extended the hand of friendship to all true believers in Christ.

"It is surely our duty to confess everywhere and always that we are first Christians, and only secondly Baptists. The tie which binds us to Christ is more important in our eyes than that which binds us to those of the same faith and order. We live in hope that the Spirit of Christ in us, and in all other Christian bodies, may induce such growth of mind and heart that the sense of unity in Christ may not only overtop and hide the fences of division, but may ultimately do away with these fences altogether."[4]

Brethren. Unity in diversity. This is the essence of Christian freedom.

---

4. *Baptists of the World, 1905–1970* (Ft. Worth: Southern Baptists' Radio and Television Commission, 1970), p. 94.

Bibliography

Barclay, William. *The Letters to the Galatians and Ephesians.* Philadelphia: The Westminster Press, 1958.

Blackwelder, Oscar F. "The Epistle to the Galatians." *The Interpreter's Bible,* vol. 10. Nashville: Abingdon Press, 1953.

Burton, Ernest DeWitt. *A Critical and Exegetical Commentary on the Epistle to the Galatians.* International Critical Commentary. Edinburgh: T. and T. Clark, 1921.

Calvin, John. *Commentaries on the Epistles of Paul to the Galatians and Ephesians.* Grand Rapids: Wm. B. Eerdmans Publishing Co., 1957.

Coad, F. Roy. "The Letter to the Galatians." *A New Testament Commentary.* Edited by G. C. D. Howley, F. F. Bruce, and H. L. Ellison. Grand Rapids: Zondervan Publishing House, 1969.

Criswell, W. A. *Expository Sermons on Galatians.* Grand Rapids: Zondervan Publishing House, 1973.

Duncan, George S. *The Epistle of Paul to the Galatians.* Moffatt New Testament Commentary. New York: Harper and Bros., n. d.

Fields, W. C. "Galatians." In *The Teacher's Bible Commentary.* H. Franklin Paschall and Herschel H. Hobbs, gen. eds. Nashville: Broadman Press, 1972.

Findlay, George G. "The Epistle to the Galatians." In *The International Standard Bible Encyclopaedia.* Grand Rapids: Wm. B. Eerdmans Publishing Co., 1949.

Guthrie, Donald. *The Pauline Epistles.* New Testament Introduction, 3 vols. Chicago: Inter-Varsity Press, 1961.

Hamilton, Floyd E. *The Epistle to the Galatians.* Grand Rapids: Baker Book House, 1959.

Kümmel, Werner Georg. *Introduction to the New Testament.* Nashville: Abingdon Press, 1965.

Lightfoot, J. B. *The Epistle of St. Paul to the Galatians.* Reprint. Grand Rapids: Zondervan Publishing House, n.d.

MacGorman, John William. *Galatians.* The Broadman Bible Commentary, vol. 11. Nashville: Broadman Press, 1971.

McNeile, A. H. *An Introduction to the Study of the New Testament.* Oxford: Clarendon Press, 1953.

Rendall, Frederic. "The Epistle of Paul to the Galatians." In *The Expositor's Greek Testament,* vol. 3. Grand Rapids: Wm. B. Eerdmans Publishing Co., 1951.

Robertson, A. T. *Word Pictures in the New Testament,* 4 vols. Nashville: Broadman Press, 1931.

Stamm, Raymond T. "The Epistle to the Galatians." *The Interpreter's Bible,* vol. 10. Nashville: Abingdon Press, 1953.